LEARNING TO STUDY

the first steps
by
Graham Gibbs

Acknowledgements

Copyright © 1981 National Extension College Trust Ltd. Reprinted with amendments 1993.

ISBN: 0 86082 246 X

Printed by NEC Print
Design: Cover David Cutting Graphics
        Text Peter Hall
Photographs: Peter Walmsley

The National Extension College is an educational trust and a registered charity with a distinguished body of trustees. It is an independent, self-financing organisation. Since it was established in 1963, NEC has pioneered the development of flexible learning for adults. NEC is actively developing innovative materials and systems for distance learning options on over 100 courses, from basic skills and general education to degree and professional training.

For further details of NEC resources and supported courses, contact Customer Services
National Extension College Trust Ltd
18 Brooklands Avenue
Cambridge CB2 2HN
Tel. 0223 358295 Fax 0223 313586

About the author
While Graham Gibbs was writing this course he was Head of the Study Methods Group in the Institute of Educational Technology at the Open University. He was undertaking research into how Open University students go about their studies. He is now a Principal Lecturer at Oxford Polytechnic and Head of the Education Methods Unit. He studied Psychology at City University and at University College London. He has run courses in study methods in many universities, polytechnics and colleges and written a book for teachers on how to run such courses which is used all over the world. He was born in 1950 and has one daughter and a crazy dog.

CONTENTS

Pages

Introduction to the Course   5

1   What this course is about   7

2   Explaining yourself in writing   17
    Being evaluative   23

3   Planning   33
    Being knowledgeable and thinking straight   42

4   Remembering   49

5   How do you learn best?   61

6   Getting organised, getting down to it and sticking at it   69

    Epilogue   83

Learning to Study is now only available from the National Extension College for self study. This means that although you may wish to complete the assignments in the book for your own benefit, please do not send them to our address as we are unable to accept them for tutor marking. If you are working through a school or college, consult your teacher or tutor about whether to submit the assignments to them for marking.

Introduction to the course

This isn't simply a book to be read. It's a *course*. It's divided up into *units* which should be tackled in order. There are *six* units.

If this is the first course you've studied, or if you are doing another course at the same time, then I think it would be reasonable to expect to spend one week on each unit. Units 2 and 3, however, are twice as long as the others, and two weeks seems a reasonable target for completion of each of these. This adds up to *eight* weeks to complete the whole course. If you put in a couple of hours a week on a regular basis you could, therefore, expect to have it finished in two months.

Exactly how many hours you spend on each unit depends on you. As I said, this isn't simply a book to be *read*: there are *activities* and *assignments* too. *Activities* suggest things you can *do* which will help you to get more out of the course. Most of them ask you to write something, and then go on to show you other possible alternatives so that you can compare your own opinions with others. Obviously you can simply not bother to do the activities or write anything and just read what others have written. But you will probably get a lot more out of the course if you tackle each problem yourself before looking at other possible answers. There are several activities in each unit.

Assignments are extended activities, but when you've written them, you send them to your tutor for comments and suggestions. There are examples of other students' assignments, and tutors' replies, so you can see the sort of thing students write and the comments tutors make. There are no marks awarded and no right and wrong answers, so you need not worry about 'failing'! There are six assignments, one or two for each unit except Unit 4. This is to give you a break in the middle of the course.

There is a plan of the course, at the back, so you can see at a glance what it looks like and what it involves. I suggest you have a quick look at it now.

There are just two other points to be made in introducing this course. Firstly, it is *your* course to do with as you please. If you don't like a unit, or get stuck on it, then feel free to leave it out. If you don't want to do an assignment, feel free to go on without attempting it. If there are particular problems arising from your assignments, tell your tutor what they are. Your tutor is there to help you, so use him/her in whatever way *you* choose.

Secondly, this course is intended to be interesting — even *intriguing* — to work through. I hope you enjoy it: it's not meant to be just a hard slog. If you find it interesting enough to talk to your husband or wife, friend or workmate about ideas it has sparked off in you, then I shall have achieved my aim. I'm mainly concerned in interesting you in thinking about how you study.

UNIT 1: What this course is about

This course is different

Unlike many courses, this course contains no facts which you must learn and which I will then test your memory of. In some History courses you have to learn dates of battles, in most Physics courses you have to memorise formulae, and in all French courses you have to memorise vocabulary. But this course is different. In fact, there aren't any 'right answers' at all! Instead, what I have tried to do in writing this course is to help you to *think* about studying – about what it will involve, what demands it will make on you, and about how you can use your abilities to meet those demands.

This course will *not* involve your practising impressive-looking study techniques which will stretch your eyes so that you can read faster, or miraculously improve your memory. The sort of claims made for the effectiveness of study techniques are often fraudulent. And in any case the difference between sophisticated, effective students and inefficient beginners is largely *not* to do with their study techniques. Instead, it is to do with how organised they are, and how well they understand what they are doing in studying. Sophisticated students are aware of their own studying and can talk about why they are taking their notes in the way they are, or why they are reading in a particular way.

Studying isn't complicated

Studying is not an impossibly difficult activity – it's largely straightforward and involves common sense. However, at school most of us were not encouraged to use our common sense in our learning. In fact, we were not encouraged to think about how or why we were doing what we were doing at all – we just got on with it in the way we were told to.

When we return to learning many years later, most of us have only a very limited range of study *habits*. I call them 'habits' because we use them thoughtlessly and because we have never done anything else. And many of these habits are quite inappropriate for adult learning.

What *Learning to Study* is about is going beyond these limited habits, becoming aware of *what* we are doing in studying and *why*, and using our common sense to make sensible decisions about *how* to go about doing it.

There are no simple rules to help you

There are no short cuts to this awareness or to making sensible decisions about how to study. There are no simple rules to learn or procedures to follow which will automatically result in more effective studying. What is more, improvements will tend to come rather slowly, and largely as a consequence of actually studying, and seeing what is working and what isn't. For example, it is difficult to know how best to go about taking notes while you are reading unless you are reading something and seeing what sort of note-taking helps most. So there are limits to what this course can achieve until you are also studying another course.

So what can this course do for you?

I've written this course with six main aims in mind:

(i)   To reassure you that you will be able to study and benefit from studying.

(ii) To give you a realistic impression of what studying will be like, and what it will involve — so that you will know what to expect, what difficulties you will face, and how to overcome them.

(iii) To convince you that you can already do most of the things which studying will demand of you, to explain what these things are, and to show that studying does *not* involve an entirely new range of skills beyond your current experience.

(iv) To help you to find out about yourself as a learner and to recognise what sort of studying works for you.

(v)   To help you to think about organising yourself to fit studying into your life and to get it done when you need to.

(vi) To help you to use correspondence courses to the best advantage. In particular, this will mean using your tutor in a way which helps you, and getting used to learning on your own.

ACTIVITY 1

Have a quick look through this course and see if you can see where I try to achieve these aims. Fill in this table as far as you can. Then turn to my table and see where *I* think I'm trying to achieve them.

Aims	Which units try to achieve these aims?
(i) (ii) (iii) (iv) (v) (vi)	

Well, you probably found some of the aims easier to locate than others! This is what *I* think I'm doing in this course:

Aims	
(i) (ii)	Both these aims are tackled in Unit 1
(iii)	Units 2, 3 and 4
(iv)	Unit 5
(v)	Unit 6
(vi)	Throughout the entire course! (but particularly in the assignments)

If this doesn't match up with your opinion, have another look through the course and see if you can see why not. There is certainly room for disagreement, but it is probably helpful for you to know what I think I'm trying to achieve at any particular point, even if you don't agree!

Are you the right sort of person to be studying this course?
One way of answering this question is to look at what other people studying with the National Extension College are like. A little over half are women — about a third of whom are housewives. About three quarters are between 20 and 45 years old and one in ten is over 55. Nearly a half finished their full-time education at 16 years old or younger and only a half have the equivalent of more than four 'O' levels. I asked some of the students who were about to start this course to describe themselves, and to try to explain to me why they were starting to study at all. Here are some of their answers:

'I am a middle-aged housewife with a husband and two teenage children. I am not out at work and so rather housebound. I have always attended Workers' Education Association classes and preferably day-time classes which are increasingly hard to find. A friend started the Open University which made me think I would enjoy a more structured course in which I had to do work as compared to just attending a class and reading.'

'I am 32 years old, of average intelligence, married with two children, aged 9 and 12. I am employed as a TV engineer in the rental industry and have been for the last 14 years. I have attended secondary school, with further education at a Technical College. The only qualifications I hold at present are City and Guilds TV servicing. I intend to increase my understanding of technology and obtain better qualifications to aid myself with my employment prospects.'

'Married, 25, one child. Felt I needed more education. Wanted to follow my interests more closely and found some text books hard to follow.'

I also asked these students:

'Why are you studying *this* course? What do you hope to get out of it?'

ACTIVITY 2
Before you go on and read what others say about this, try writing down your own answer, as if you were trying to explain yourself to me. If you find this difficult, have a word with your husband, wife, or a friend and try to explain to them. Then write down the main things you talked about. Try to do this before you read on.

Here are three of the answers students gave me. Do they have similar reasons to your own?

'I chose this course for two reasons. First, to learn about how to study as I was never given any help on this at school, and hope it will help me with further courses. Secondly, to test myself on a short course to see if I enjoyed studying at home on my own and if I could organise myself to do it before tackling any longer course of study.'

'I am hoping to broaden my mental horizons and prevent my mind from seizing up in middle age!'

'I hope this course will give me the confidence to determinedly put pen to paper, making my mind more active, having to consciously think about things rather than just drift alone. I hope the course will help me discipline myself for further study.'

From records of all students with the National Extension College, we know that about half want to go on to study with the Open University. About a quarter say that they are studying out of interest, and about one in five want to change their career. The most common reason for studying by correspondence is that people say that they prefer to work in their own time, at their own pace and in their own home. Family responsibilities and job constraints are the other main reasons people give. But there are lots of other reasons too, so whoever you are, there will almost certainly be someone else rather like you studying this course!

How do you feel about starting to study?
Having seen what some other people think about studying, how do *you* feel about starting? What expectations do you have?

ACTIVITY 3

Set out below are a number of statements made by students just about to start studying. For each statement write down your immediate reactions to it. Does the statement fit you perfectly? In what way do you differ from the students who made these statements? Being clear in your own mind about these matters will help you do the Assignment for this first unit.

1. 'I have difficulty getting my thoughts on to paper, and writing them down.'
2. 'I'm worried that I've not used my brain for so long that it's seized up completely.'
3. 'I'm not sure just how clever I am – what I'll be able to manage and what I won't.'
4. 'I can't really see where I'm going to find the time to study.'
5. 'Family problems don't worry me. They'll have to like it or lump it.'
6. 'I don't know what the standard will be like – how hard the courses will be.'
7. 'I hope I'll get more confident as time goes on.'
8. 'I'm not looking forward to having to write to my tutor!'
9. 'I'm no good at sums and maths – I hope I'm not expected to do any.'
10. 'I'm a bit hesitant about *this* course. I don't know what I'm likely to get out of it.'

What will studying be like?

I asked some National Extension College students:

'How have you fitted studying into your everyday life?'

Their answers may give you some indication of what you will find:

'Life is now a timetable. There is a time for everything. A time to earn bread. A time to eat. A time to study. A time to sleep. A time to relax. Like an efficient railway system I do my best to keep to the timetable. I am seen less about the house but I have an understanding wife. At least she knows where I am at particular times. I am in the study.'

'In my view this is the most difficult aspect of the course. I had to explain to my wife and children that there would be certain times when I must be left alone and would not be able to join them in play or conversation. I had to get them to accept the fact that I wished to study and take an interest in the progress of my studies. We are a close family and do a great deal together so that it was not easy to opt out of my usual role of husband and father for two hours each night. I feel that whatever determination the student must have, his family must match this and in addition provide encouragement and understanding. The course may be hard for the student but it can be hell for his family.'

'Quite well after a few teething problems. No family problems as my parents are very understanding. I have had to stay in a few nights a week so I do not get to the pub so much.'

I also asked them what changes had taken place in their lives since they had started studying:

'In many ways I have felt happier and more fulfilled as a result of studying. At the end of the day something constructive has been achieved and although time-consuming is a very satisfying way of filling one's time.'

'My own free time has become much more ordered so that the study periods can be provided for each day. I find that I can now complete all manner of household tasks more easily as my time is properly planned. However, I do have a "slobs day" from time to time – nothing planned or organised. I just do as I please!'

'I am becoming more organised. All time is now valuable. It is too precious to waste a minute. I think I am turning into a question mark. Other people's opinions are no longer passively accepted. Silent cries of "I do not agree" very often flit through my mind.'

What difficulties are you likely to face?
Even successful students, managing perfectly well, have difficulties. You are bound to have some too. These, described by students, are some you might run into:

'The only real difficulties are personal ones, particularly in adhering to a timetable. It all looks good on paper, but actually being allowed by family commitments to stick to it is a different matter.'

'The only problem is I shall always be lazy, I think.'

'Difficulties:
1 Making and keeping the allotted *time* to study, which is essential.
2 Trying to feel strongly that what you are doing is as important as all the other trivia of living.
3 Trying not to feel guilty at what is rather a selfish activity.'

'The only difficulty I have found is having to write and write until I reach the target of 500-700 words. This is not because I do not have much to write about, more the opposite in my case, I tend to write too much. I try not to repeat myself and this leads to boredom, frustration and loss of interest. My tutor informed me that it was not necessary to write more than I reasonably felt I could say.'

'Difficulties: finding somewhere, and *time*, to study without distractions. Also for quiet reading. Getting back into the system of studying after a break of several years.'

12

Finally, I've selected some more quotes from students who have been studying on their own for a while. I asked them:

'What advice, warning or encouragement would you like to give to a student just about to start studying?'

I was very impressed by how seriously the students took this question. Here is some of their advice:

'Don't try to do too much. Starting with five hours' study a week and building up to ten is better than starting with 15 hours and collapsing in a heap. Learn how to switch off the television set. Make a special effort to be nice to your wife/husband. You will need her/his help. Find someone to talk to about your subject; anyone will do. Keep asking questions. Stay curious. Don't day-dream about study. Sit down and start writing!'

'(a) Discuss your plans with the family and get them on your side. Do not neglect their needs and isolate yourself too much from them.
(b) Plan your studying.
(c) Do not be over-ambitious, be realistic.
(d) Enjoy it! NEC courses are well run and your tutors are all friendly people. If some schools for children had the same attitude to learning, they would have to force the children to leave!'

'Really stick at it. If you feel yourself not wanting to do it, will yourself on. Do use a quiet place if possible — distractions are lethal.'

'Firstly, to examine their reasons for studying thoroughly. Do it for their own sake, not to please parents or bosses, or it will all become a complete burden. Secondly, have a bash at everything; there's nothing to lose.'

'1 It is very important to make out a timetable and stick to it — once you get behind, it is very difficult to catch up.
2 Try to get family and friends to help you and encourage you. Also, if you can study with a friend, it helps you to keep at it, especially through difficult parts.
3 Don't give up if it seems difficult. There are other students with the same problems — talk it over with them — see if you can sort the problems together.'

And just to prove that I am not taking an unrealistically positive view of things:

'I think that studying at home is only to be encouraged if there really are no other options. I'm sure that full-time study at University or College would be preferable, as this does not require *quite* as much self-discipline and organisation.'

ASSIGNMENT A

I'd like you to write a letter to your tutor and introduce yourself. Describe yourself and your situation.

1. Why do you want to study?
2. What are you hoping to get out of this course?
3. What do you ultimately want to get out of studying?
4. What problems do you think you'll have in getting started on your studies?
5. What changes do you expect to take place in your life as a result of fitting studying in?
6. What practical steps do you intend taking in order to help you study?
7. How did you find Unit 1?
8. How do you feel about the whole business of studying?

There are three main purposes in your writing this letter:

(a) You should be aiming to establish a useful working relationship with your tutor. Your tutor is there to help you, so use him or her in whatever way you think will help you most. Set the tone for how you want to carry on.

(b) You should be using this exercise to help you get your thoughts straight. Look back through this unit and remind yourself how you reacted to things and what you thought. Note down the thoughts you had which you think are important to you. You may perhaps like to use my list of questions above to help you *structure* your thoughts.

(c) You should be aiming to give a clear impression of yourself, and of your thoughts and feelings about studying, to your tutor. The better your tutor knows and understands you, the more use he or she will be to you.

Your tutor will then write back, introduce himself or herself, and make some comments and observations about what you have written.

Here is an example of a student's letter to his tutor:

> 25 Talbots House,
> Heatherfield Road,
> Luton.
> 10.5.81

Dear Mrs Phillips,

I'm writing to introduce myself as one of your students. I've just finished reading Unit 1 and I'm going to try to write this letter at one sitting or I'll never get round to finishing it! I'm going to use the questions in the order they are listed on page 10 or I won't know where to start or what to write about next.

I'm a Post Office worker. I'm 35. I live in a small flat with my wife and one child, Pat, who is nine. My wife works down at the Co-op, only part-time so she can be at home when Pat gets home from school.

There are lots of training schemes and exams and things if you want to get on in the Post Office. At least that's what it seems. I joined without any background and I'm getting fed up with my work. It's not bad work, not dirty and it's indoors, but I'm sure I could manage a lot better. So, now Pat's growing up I thought I'd see if I could improve myself — maybe get on to a different grade and do something more challenging. I didn't fancy getting straight on to a training course and finding I couldn't cope — specially as there'd be people who'd know me — so I thought I'd try something on my own first and test myself out. I saw this advert in the paper so I wrote off.

I didn't have any trouble reading Unit 1 and I found all the things the other students said very interesting. I showed some of them to my wife. I don't think we'd really discussed what effect it would have if I started spending time studying. I hadn't really thought about it. It hasn't hit us yet but I suppose it will do, as I need to put more time in. I'm going to try to get Unit 2 done in two weeks. I've had a quick look at it and it seems to be a bit longer than Unit 1.

Yours sincerely,
Sean Ryan

ACTIVITY 4

If you were Sean Ryan's tutor, Mrs Phillips, what would you think of this letter, and of Sean? Read the letter again and write down whatever you think of.

I don't know what Mrs Phillips would think, but these are the things *I* wrote down as I re-read the letter:

1 The first bit seems a very nice introduction. It's very chatty and frank. He says what he's going to write about in the letter — he's going to follow the list of questions. That'll help me follow what he says.
2 Well, he *started* following the questions, then he seemed to drift off a bit. He never seems to get back to the questions either.
3 I'm getting a very clear impression of *why* he's taking the course. I wonder what it is he's worried he won't be good at? Is it reading, writing, or what?
4 He doesn't actually seem to have taken any steps yet to organise himself, though he expects he'll have to. I wonder what his wife thinks about it?

I think if I were Mrs Phillips, I would wish Sean had kept to the list of questions and possibly been a bit more detailed. That way I would have found out a bit more about his studying. But overall I'd be happy enough. Sean seems to be getting on OK, has written to me, his tutor, and seems to have at least an informal plan (to complete Unit 2 in a fortnight) to continue. He's being very open about things, so I wouldn't be worried that he's covering up any problems. I'd ask him a few more questions and hope he'd answer them with his next assignment.

UNIT 2: Explaining yourself in writing

Introduction

This unit contains two sections: 'Explaining yourself in writing' and 'Being evaluative'. This first section is six pages long, has four activities and one assignment. Section 2 is eight pages long and has three activities and one assignment. Try to complete these two sections in two weeks. Set yourself deadlines for sending the assignments to your tutor, and try to keep to them.

EXPLAINING YOURSELF IN WRITING

When you are following a course, you are usually asked to *write* things, whether it is 'essays', 'assignments', 'reports' or whatever. What use is it to *you* if you write something and send it to your tutor? Even on courses where there is an exam at the end (for example, an O-level course), the writing you do *during* the course won't usually count towards your qualification — so why do it at all?

ACTIVITY 5

Write down all the reasons you can think of for bothering to *write* things on a course.

I don't expect you to see things in exactly the same way as I do, but see how your reasons compare with mine:

1   *Getting practice at writing.*
If you take an exam, it will most probably be a written exam. Whether you have to write very short answers or long 'essay' answers, you'll benefit from practice in writing them. For me this is possibly the *least* important reason for writing during the course.

2   *Getting feedback from your tutor*
By seeing your written work your tutor can let you know what he thinks you understand well and what you seem to misunderstand, have got wrong, or missed out. It is sometimes difficult to tell whether what you are learning is the right thing, whether you are learning *enough* (or in *too much* detail) and whether you

understand the topic properly. If you write down what you do understand and know about the topic, your tutor will be able to advise you.

There is an important difference here from what you probably did at school when you wrote things for teachers. If you were like me, you were trying to cover up what you didn't understand and to give as exaggerated an impression as possible of what you knew. My own aim at school was to avoid low marks and to avoid being criticised as lazy or stupid. But now, as an adult learner, your aim is quite different – it is to *learn*. So in your writing it will be most useful for you deliberately to *expose* what it is you don't know, and to give your tutor a realistic impression of how you are managing. If your tutor can see what you are having trouble with, he can help you with it. This is obviously very different from what you would do in an exam, where you would be trying to look as impressive as possible and not let the examiner see what you don't know. This means that in the writing you do during a course you have a choice. Either you can practice being impressive for the exams, or you can concentrate on writing in a way which will result in your learning more. The choice is yours.

As a teacher I am mainly interested in students *learning*, and so it is vital to me that my students are able to explain themselves in writing. If they explain themselves very poorly, then I can't tell what they know and understand and what they don't, and so I can't be very helpful to them.

3   *Writing to develop your ideas*

Students very often find that they remember and understand best those parts of a course they wrote essays or reports about. The effort involved in organising your thoughts and expressing them in detail in writing seems to be one of the very best ways of learning. It's rather like teaching. If you really want to understand something and to learn about it, then try teaching it to somebody – a workmate or friend. Writing can be like teaching. What you are trying to do is *explain yourself* in writing. For me this is the most important reason for writing. If I want to get to grips with a new topic – an educational theory I don't know much about or a teaching method I've never used – one of the ways I learn about it is to *write* about it. I choose an audience – often my colleagues at work – then I try to explain to them what I think this theory, or teaching method or whatever, is really about. If I don't understand it, then this soon becomes apparent to me when I find I can't explain myself in writing. It is hard to get away with vague and muddled thinking in writing and still manage to explain yourself!

So I think explaining yourself in writing is very important in studying. But what does it involve? People often have rather grand expectations of 'academic' writing. They think it should involve all sorts of formal and pompous turns of phrase: 'It is believed that . . . . .' and 'The author would like to reserve his judgement'. They think that it should use long technical terms and look as obscure and unreadable as possible. Of course, exactly the opposite is true. The basic principles of good, clear explanations are the same whether you are directing a stranger to the railway station or writing an academic paper for a learned journal. If you use your common sense, you can give a very clear explanation to the stranger — and you can explain yourself in writing in the same way. Does this sound absurd? I'll see if I can persuade you!

I live in a small village in Warwickshire called Eathorpe. I'm going to imagine that you have stopped at my door and asked to get to the nearest railway station. I scratch my head, point down the road and say:

> 'Go down there till you get to the end, then veer left by the farm and go straight on over the brick bridge, that's after about 50 yards, probably less, say 40 yards. There's a bench by a gate. Can't miss it! Go up the hill straight ahead of you to Johnson's farm and down the other side. Then it gets windy. There will probably be some sheep in the field — that's on the other side from the big house. It's got ivy all over it. The bus stop is near there. Then you come to another road. It's a bit confusing. The road comes from over the *other* hill. I think you'd better ask from there.'

ACTIVITY 6

What's wrong with these instructions? If you were to feel confident of getting to the nearest station, what would you rather I'd told you and how, and what would you rather I'd left out? Write your answer down before reading on.

I gave this explanation of how to get to the nearest railway station to a friend at work, Alistair, and asked him the same question about it as I have just asked you. Alistair's reply went something like this:

> 'My mind just goes blank when people explain things to me like that. It's all details — masses of them which I can't imagine and can't remember. Most of the details are too vague to be helpful anyway. What's worse is that I've still got no idea where the railway station is! Even if I managed to go wherever it is you're taking me to, I wouldn't know where I was then!'

Many students' essays are just like the explanation! They go straight into minute details which are hard to follow. I've no idea where these essays are taking me and, even if I *can* wade through them, I've no idea where I've been taken to when I reach the end! All such essays consist of is a kaleidoscope of largely irrelevant observations which seem to have been included in the order in which the students thought of them.

I'll now try giving you a rather *different* explanation of how to get to the nearest railway station from my house. Is this explanation better?

> 'It's in Leamington. Go to Wappenbury and get on to the Rugby road. You go through several places like Weston and Cubbington. Go down the Parade and it's off Lower Warwick Road.'

ACTIVITY 7

What do you think of *this* explanation? Write down your comments before reading on.

Alistair's comment was:

> 'Look Graham, I don't even know how to get to Wappenbury or on to the Rugby road, wherever that is. Even if I got myself into Leamington, how would I find the Parade, or get to Lower Warwick Road? I know you've given me the facts, but that doesn't help me much I'm afraid — you'll have to explain how I'm to *use* them — how they link together. And before you start doing that, what sort of a journey am I letting myself in for? Can I *walk* there? And supposing I got lost and couldn't find Cubbington, What would I do then?'

I've also seen lots of students' essays which closely resemble this second explanation. They are very bald and matter-of-fact and tend to be rather short. The students who wrote them think they've said all that needs to be said. They've included the main facts, so what else is there to do? They don't seem to realise that I'm not very familiar with what they are writing about. Presumably they know a very great deal more than their essays reveal: just as I know a great deal more about the journey to Leamington station than this second explanation reveals. I have assumed you already know about the Rugby road, and the streets of Leamington. I have assumed you know that Leamington is about six miles away. It is a very poor explanation of what I know, because I didn't think about what *you* needed to know — in fact, I didn't think much at all!

So this time I'll try to get it right! I'll try to give an explanation which you can make sense of and follow without trouble. Here goes:

> 'Leamington is the nearest railway station. This is the River Leam which runs on into Leamington about six miles over that way to the East. It will take you about 20 minutes by car. There is no public transport. There is a main road near here which goes to Leamington, so I'll divide the journey up into three sections: getting to the main road; taking the main road to Leamington; and finding the station once you're in Leamington.
>
> If you follow the road you are on in the direction you are faacing for about a mile, you will come to the main road. You go over this hill here and the main road is the first road you come to.
>
> At the T-junction with the main road, there will be a signpost saying *left* to Leamington. The main road is fairly winding and you go through several villages before coming to the outskirts of Leamington. You will recognise Leamington by the housing estates.
>
> Follow the signposts to the town centre. You have got to get on to the

Parade which runs through the middle of town. The road you will be on is parallel with the Parade, which will be one block to your right. Take any of the turnings to your right and you'll come to the Parade. Turn left on to it, and go downhill to the bottom end of town. When you pass under an iron railway bridge, turn right and the station is on your right.'

ACTIVITY 8

What are the main characteristics of this explanation which you would find helpful in getting to the station? Write down what you think *before* reading what I've got to say about it —so you can compare you views with my own.

When I gave this third explanation to Alistair, he said:

'This is much more helpful. Right at the start you've given me a general idea of what the journey would entail. Knowing roughly where Leamington is made it much easier to make sense of the rest of the explanation. And dividing the journey up into three bits and then dealing with these separately made it much easier to think about and remember.

There seems to be about the right amount of detail too — just enough so that I'll know what to do, but not so much that I'll get confused or lose sight of the general direction I'm going in.

Also, I was just thinking "How will I know if I'm lost or whether I've already got to Leamington?" when you told me I'd recognise Leamington by the housing estates. That's just the sort of check I needed.

I suspect I'll find Leamington a bit harder to find my way around than your explanation suggests. Is it that you don't know Leamington very well, or had you just decided you'd given me enough to get by?'

I can see in this third explanation many of the characteristics of good essays, good reports, in fact, of any clear piece of writing:

1   It tells you at the start what you are in for and what the *structure* of the explanation is going to be — like any good introduction.
2   It divides the explanation up into sections which makes it easier to follow. This is the reason for planning and structuring an essay.
3   It includes neither too much nor too little detail.
4   It doesn't make any unjustified assumptions about what the reader already knows.
5   It lets the reader check whether he's on the right track or not from time to time and tells him where he's being taken next. It might have done rather more of this by, for example, saying: 'At this point you will have completed the first two sections of the journey, and all you have to do now is find your way across Leamington to the station'.

All these points are simply a consequence of bearing the *reader's* needs in mind. If you forget these points, then you may not enable your reader to understand what you know.

There have been additional advantages for me in taking these points into account in giving you instructions to get to the nearest station.

1   It's made me think about the journey, and what I know about it rather more carefully than I have done before. I'd never though of it in three sections until I wrote the third explanation. Trying to explain myself helped me to *organise* what I knew.

2   When someone asks me the same question again (or even a similar question, such as: 'How do I get from my house in Leamington to your house in Eathorpe?') I now have a ready-made framework for an answer. I don't have to think about it from scratch every time.

3   The third explanation can help me learn more about the journey to Leamington. If someone who is much more familiar than I am with this journey were to read my explanation, he could see whether I'd got it right and, by being able to see what I know, suggest improvements: some details perhaps, or a different and even clearer way of dividing up the journey and explaining it. Had this 'expert' seen only my second explanation, he wouldn't have been able to tell what I knew and what I didn't, and wouldn't have known what advice to offer to improve my understanding of the journey.

So if you can give clear directions to a stranger about how to get to the railway station, then you know how to write good explanations. All you have to do is:

1   Let your reader know where you're taking him.
2   Divide your explanation up into sections and let your reader know what these sections will be.
3   Avoid confusing your reader with too many detailed observations along the way.
4   Assume your reader knows nothing about the area.
5   Remind your reader where he is from time to time — where you've brought him from and where you are taking him next.

ASSIGNMENT B
Write your tutor an explanation of how to get to your house from your nearest railway station. Try to bear in mind the five points I've listed above. When you have finished writing this explanation, try to write some comments on what you have done. For example, you may have used some other useful devices for helping your tutor to follow your explanation which I have not thought of using. Or you may feel that a part of your explanation might cause your tutor problems. In your comments, try to point these things out, and to explain why you

think your explanation is clear (or unclear!). You might like to try your instructions out on a friend first to see what he says! Then send your instructions *and* your comments to your tutor.

BEING EVALUATIVE

In our everyday lives we evaluate things all the time. We decide whether we like people and want to be friendly with them. We decide whether to buy a loaf of *Mother's Pride* or *Sunblest*, a packet of cornflakes or *Shreddies*. Sometimes these evaluative judgements are intuitive and we are never conscious of making them. Sometimes they are very deliberate and take into account various pieces of evidence about the things we're evaluating. The *Mother's Pride* loaf may be bigger and 2p cheaper, but the *Sunblest* loaf is crustier and tends to go stale less quickly, for example. In many academic topics the things you're learning about are very complex and there is lots of evidence to take into account in order to evaluate different arguments.

At school I was taught that the causes of the French Revolution were . . . . . . and I was given a list of ten causes to learn. Churning these ten out in my O-level history exam was sufficient to pass the exam. But as an adult learner what I am concerned about is which of these 'causes' really were causes? Were they all equally important? Were they related to each other? If I were asked to identify the two most important factors which gave rise to the French Revolution, which would I choose and why? In other words, I would be concerned not just to list these 'causes' but to *evaluate* them. Evaluating the causes of the French Revolution is obviously a very complicated business, but it isn't any different in substance to what we do in our everyday lives. In fact, in our everyday lives we are seldom as daft as to do the sort of thing I did for my history O-level. Let me illustrate this.

I'd like you to imagine two football supporters sitting together in a pub the day after Nottingham Forest knocked Liverpool out of the League Cup in February 1980. One of them thinks Forest is the better team, while the other thinks Liverpool is better.

F.   See the match last night?

L.   Yeah, travesty wasn't it?

F.   What do you mean 'travesty'?

L.   Absolute travesty; I've never seen a side so outplayed, and still win. They were so lucky.

F.   That wasn't luck: Forest defended well, and there was nothing Liverpool could do to get through that defence. The only luck Forest had was that Liverpool thought they could win by rushing at them for ninety minutes.

L.   That's rubbish! You had a penalty – it should never have been given. Nine times out of ten you'd never get away with tactics like that. You just got all the lucky breaks. You were outplayed and fluked your way through.

F.   Just like we did last season when we beat you in the European Cup, I suppose?

L.   I know it sounds like sour grapes, but Graeme Souness was right in the interview after the game. You could never match Liverpool for ability. You just pack your defence, sit tight in your own half and let Liverpool come at you, and hope that you might break away and snatch the odd goal.

F.   But it worked didn't it? And it's the results that matter.

L.   Is it hell — there's no skill there. You just bore the pants off everyone. You don't offer anything to the game. And it *doesn't* work; that's why we're top of the League, and you're half way down the table.

F.   We were League champions last season, and we're not that far behind you this season. There's still a long way to go, and we can play a bit too when we have to.

L.   I suppose that's why you get 25,000 and think it's a good crowd. At Anfield we start worrying if we get less than 40,000 on Saturday afternoon. Cup ties and they're queuing across Stanley Park. That's a sign of whether you're playing football or not — whether anyone wants to come and watch.

F.   That's just because you've got a tradition of football at Liverpool which we haven't got at Nottingham yet. In any case, that just makes Forest's recent achievements even more outstanding. At Liverpool your gate receipts must be twice what Forest's are. You can afford big wages for the reserves, and can buy who you want at whatever price.

L   *We* aren't the ones who splash out money all over the place trying to buy success instead of earning it through creating your own team.

F.   And I suppose your Dalglish and Souness came up through the apprentices? We've got just as many people in the team as you who've come through the apprentices. Also a lot of our first team are players no one else wanted, who came for a song, and Clough and Taylor managed to turn them into part of a team that won the European Cup. There's nothing wrong with buying good players to bring you success, provided you can keep them playing well when you've got them.

L.   Like Francis, I suppose? He's done nothing since you bought him. What a waste of money!

F.   But he scored the winning goal against Malmo in the European Cup! I was thinking of Shilton too — he's come right back into the reckoning for the England keeper's place.

L.   Rubbish! He's not in the same league as Ray Clemence.

F.   What old 'Through-the-legs' Clemence?

L.   When Shilton was playing for England, he let in so many soft goals they dropped him. There's not one position in the team where a Forest player is as good as a Liverpool one. We've got the better forwards, midfield defence, goal keeper, *and* manager. . . . .

F.   You think Bob Paisley's a better manager than Brian Clough or Peter Taylor?

L.   That's just it. You've got two together who're not as good as Bob Paisley.

F.   You think Bob Paisley, who inherited a squad who were already champions, and who just kept them chugging along, is a better manager than one who's taken a team from the Second Division to be European Cup winners in four seasons?

L.   Listen, if you want to look at records, look at Liverpool's Football League champions practically every other year since 1970; F.A. Cup winners a couple of times; retained the European Cup: that's what I call a record. And Paisley's carrying on where Bill Shankley left off. You think that's easy? That's just as difficult as what Clough's done at Forest. You think Clough could have taken over at Anfield? Could he hell! There'd be just the same mess as he made at Leeds. All he can do is take over a bunch of no-hopers and scare them half to death. That'll work for a couple of seasons until they get used to it, then they'll sink back into the Second Division where they belong.

F.   Well, there's not going to be a League Cup Final win for *you* this season, that's for sure, and you're already out of the European Cup — and I reckon Forest could retain the European Cup (which they went on to do!)

Obviously such an argument could go on for ever. If you look at what they are arguing about, it centres around a number of themes: Is Liverpool's record better than Forest's? Does Liverpool attract more support than Forest? Is Liverpool's management better? Is Forest playing better at the moment, or were they just lucky on the night? and so on. In evaluating whether Liverpool is better than Forest, they looked at *evidence* along each of these themes. They didn't do it particularly systematically or thoroughly, but on the other hand, they certainly didn't simply *list* facts about their teams. Had they done so, their conversation might have gone like this:

L.   Liverpool is top of the First Division. Forest is tenth.

F.   Forest has beaten Liverpool twice this season.

L.   Liverpool gets average gates of 50,000. Forest gets average gates of 26,000.

F.   Forest won the European Cup in 1979.

L.   Liverpool won the European Cup in 1977 and 1978.

F.   Liverpool paid £400,000 for Kenny Dalglish.

L.   Forest paid £1,000,000 for Trevor Francis.

F.   Brain Clough has won the League with two different clubs.

L.   Bob Paisley has won the League three times for Liverpool.

. . . . . and so on

Obviously nobody actually argues like this. People don't just spout facts at each other. They *use* facts. They carefully select the relevant facts and argue around them. The important things are the arguments themselves. Our football supporters were not disputing the facts, but what the facts added up to, and there was plenty of scope for interpreting the facts in different ways.

25

Some of what our football supporters were saying *was* quite different from an academic evaluation.

ACTIVITY 9

What can you see in the pub discussion which you think should *not* be a part of an academic evaluation? Write down whatever you think.

My main objection to this discussion as an academic evaluation is that there are rather a lot of unsubstantiated *opinions*. For example, the Liverpool supporter said that Forest was outplayed. While it might have been possible to support this assertion with evidence of how long Liverpool was in possession of the ball, compared with Forest, he didn't offer any such evidence. So I have to assume this was just a subjective opinion and rule it out in my objective attempt to decide whether Liverpool is indeed a better side. Later on, the Liverpool supporter called both the Forest and Leeds teams, before Brian Clough took charge of them, 'no-hopers'. There is no way this sort of assertion could be supported by objective evidence. Also, some of the arguments are so superficial that it's hard to evaluate them one way or the other. Was Trevor Francis worth a million pounds? Well, one of them said he'd done nothing since he'd been bought, and the other said he scored the goal that won the European Cup Final. That's hardly enough evidence on which to base an evaluation. There are many other such examples.

So overall, though this *was* an evaluative discussion, it wasn't very academically respectable. While they didn't simply spout facts at each other, they went too far the other way and tried to draw conclusions without a sound basis in evidence, and to convince each other with mere opinions. There's more to being evaluative than having a slanging match!

ACTIVITY 10

Let's have a look at evaluation in a more 'academic' context than deciding whether Nottingham Forest is better than Liverpool. We have here two short essays written by students on a Technology course. The students were asked: 'Is Concorde noisier than ordinary jets?' The two students had both read the same newspaper articles which talked about how noisy aircraft were. The articles contained all sorts of facts and figures and discussions of these facts. What I'd like you to do is read these two essays and to write down what you think of them. Write down what you think of the first one *before* you go on to read the second. When you have finished writing down what you think of the second one, there is another activity for you to do.

Essay 1   Is Concorde noisier than ordinary jets?

The legal noise limit at Heathrow airport is 110 decibels*. The people who make Concorde say it makes a noise between 104 and 108 decibels while it is taking off. When Concorde started taking off at Heathrow, 21 out of the first 35 take-offs were louder than 110 decibels. In 1976 there were 109 infringements of Heathrow's noise limit by Concorde. In 1976 there were 1,941 infringements of Heathrow's noise limit by ordinary jets. Concorde seldom makes the 'top ten' of noisiest take-offs at Heathrow each month.

At Dulles airport in Washington, USA, Concorde averages 120 decibels at take-off. Ordinary jets average about 108 decibels. In September 1976 Concorde averaged 121 decibels while taking off from Dulles airport and there were 186 complaints. In October 1976 Concorde averaged 117 decibels and there were 101 complaints.

Opinion polls have shown a drop in opposition to Concorde. Opposition from people living around Dulles airport has dropped from 37% to 26%. Opposition from people living around Kennedy airport, New York, has dropped from 63% to 53%.

Concorde can turn away from a runway at an altitude of only 100 feet, compared with 480 feet for ordinary jets, and so can turn away from built-up areas sooner.

Now write down what you think of this essay before reading on.

Essay 2   Is Concorde noisier than ordinary jets?

Despite Concorde gradually getting quieter, and people complaining less, Concorde is still clearly noisier than ordinary jets. What is more, it is noisier than

Decibels are units of measurement of *noise* in the same way that *degrees* are units of measurement of *temperature*.

the bare figures show. There are a number of reasons for this.

Firstly, Concorde was originally compared, in 1976, largely with old-fashioned *turbo-jet* aircraft like the Boeing 707 and Trident which are very noisy. Newer aircraft use *fan jets* which are quieter. For example, the Boeing 747 jumbo jet uses fan jets and is quieter than the older 707. So today, as the older, noisier jets have stopped being used so much, so Concorde has become *comparatively* noisier.

Secondly, 'noise-meters' only register numbers of decibels, and can't indicate how 'shrill' or 'piercing' Concorde is. People's subjective descriptions of Concorde indicate that it is much more of a nuisance, even if the decible readings aren't much higher than ordinary jets.

Thirdly, measures of complaints against Concorde and opinion poll measures can't be trusted. People get used to Concorde over time even if it doesn't get quieter. Also, the people who live round airports often work there and might lose their jobs if they complained too much about noise.

Fourthly, how noisy an aircraft is at take-off depends a lot on how skilful the pilot is and how heavily loaded the plane is. Ordinary jets have been measured at twice the legal noise limit, struggling to take off while over-loaded and flown by relatively untrained pilots. In contrast, Concorde is nearly always practically empty and has specially trained highly skilled pilots. With these advantages, ordinary jets would be much quieter.

Finally, Concorde's ability to turn away from built-up areas sooner after take-off than ordinary jets also means it can turn away from the 'noise-meters' at the end of the runway!

For all these reasons Concorde is probably much noisier, in comparison with ordinary jets, than the figures indicate.

Now write down what you think of this second essay.

ACTIVITY 11

Now you have written your comments down, I'd like you to fill in this table. What do you think are the strengths and weakness of these two essays? Fill the four spaces in before reading further.

	Strengths	*Weaknesses*
Essay 1		
Essay 2		

This is what I wrote down after I had read the two essays:

Essay 1
I kept thinking 'So what?' after every new fact. This student has told me an enormous number of facts about how noisy Concorde is, and a few about how noisy it is compared with ordinary jets, but he hasn't answered the question. He ought to have *evaluated* all the facts and decided that 'yes, Concorde *is* noisier', or 'No, it isn't', or even 'It's hard to tell'. But he hasn't drawn any conclusions at all. He seems to have left all the decisions up to me, the reader. Has he assumed that I can draw my own conclusions from the facts or was he simply unable to draw any conclusions himself? There doesn't seem to be any sort of argument to it or structure – it's just a *list* of facts. It was very diligent of him to collect all these facts together, but a bit pointless – a wasted effort. I wonder if he thinks he's supposed to memorise all these facts? I hope not! But perhaps my strongest feeling about this essay is that it is terribly dull to read. I would have reluctantly given it about 5 out of 10, for conscientiousness, had I been marking it.

Essay 2
This student has gone beyond the bare facts. Instead of just listing them, she has interpreted them, evaluated them, and told me what they really mean, what it is reasonable to *conclude* from them. In fact, she both starts and finishes her essay with her conclusion: that Concorde *is* noisier. What is more, she concludes, it is even noisier than the figures show. She must have *questioned* the figures to conclude this. She hasn't just accepted all the decibel readings and told me what they were; she's looked carefully at what they mean, and whether such figures on their own give the whole picture. I find this much more interesting and informative. If someone were to ask me whether Concorde was especially noisy or not, I'd be in a much better position to give a useful answer than after reading the first essay. It looks to me as though the student who wrote this understands the issues involved better, and I would have given 9 out of 10 if I'd been marking the essay.

Were your comments similar to mine? If they were different, do we disagree with each other, or have we simply commented on different things?
This is how I filled in the table:

	Strengths	*Weaknesses*
Essay 1	Detailed Well informed Lots of evidence	Boring to read No evaluation of evidence No conclusion No structure or argument
Essay 2	Interesting arguments Went beyond evidence Clear conclusion Well structured (introduction, five points, conclusion)	No evidence to support arguments

Have I missed out things you think are important? Have you missed out things I think are important?

Conclusion

So while academic tasks usually require you to *evaluate* information, rather than just *list* it in essays or *memorise* it for tests, this is not a difficult new activity for you. You evaluate information all the time in your everyday life. However, doing it *well*, in an organised fashion which makes it clear to your listener or reader how things stand, takes practice. Here is an opportunity to practice.

ASSIGNMENT C

The following two advertisements for cars tell you all sorts of things about the cars. You may know more about them yourself. They both try to persuade you that you ought to buy them. You probably have views about what sort of car you would like, or even what makes a car a good one. If you were studying a course on what car to buy, you would probably *not* be asked a question like: 'List the characteristics of the *Cortina*'. More likely, you would be asked a question like: 'Compare and contrast the *Cortina* and the *Cavalier*'. Such a question would be asking you, in effect, to *evaluate* these two cars, given the information you have about them.

I'd like you to imagine that your tutor will give you the money to buy whichever of these cars you would prefer to own, provided you can make a convincing case to him for choosing one rather than the other. The question I would like you to write an answer to is: 'For your own personal use, is the *Cortina* a better car than the *Cavalier*?' Send your answer to your tutor.

Why can't anyone overtake the Cortina?

Many a car has challenged the Cortina.

Many a car has fallen by the wayside. Why is it that no one can even approach its popularity, let alone overtake it?

It's a question of balance.

You might find one car that can match its speed, or another that can match its space, but when you look at the whole picture – fuel economy, service costs, parts, insurance, depreciation – no car is quite so completely satisfying.

That's the genius of the Cortina, and the engineers who designed it.

It's fast but it isn't thirsty.

It's economical to run, but it isn't dull to drive.

It handles well, but it doesn't have a hard uncomfortable ride.

As a piece of engineering it's perfectly balanced.

Who can keep up with it?

By no means everyone. The Cortina has more than enough acceleration to overtake quickly and decisively on country roads. And to cruise effortlessly at motorway speed limits.

	Max speed (mph)	0–60 (secs)
Cortina 1300 single venturi	87	16.1
Cortina 1600 single venturi	94	12.7
Cortina 1600 twin venturi	101	10.9
Cortina 2000 twin venturi	105	9.8
Cortina 2300 twin venturi	109	9.6

*Ford computed performance figures for manual transmission models.

Speed isn't everything

It's no use having a high top speed if it isn't balanced by safe, predictable handling. In this department

the Cortina excels.

With front disc brakes, heavy duty front anti-roll bar, and rear gas shock absorbers standard on all models. There's an optional 'S' pack to give sports car handling characteristics for the enthusiast.

Taking some of the labour out of servicing

Bulbs can be changed without tools.
Wheel bearings need no maintenance.
Brakes are self adjusting.
Axle and gear box oil doesn't need changing.
Brake wear can be checked without removing wheels.
Clutch is self adjusting.
Check at a glance battery, brake fluid and windscreen washer bottle.

The Cortina only needs a full service once every 12,000 miles, with a minor service every 6,000 miles. Ford parts are moderately priced and the dealer network covers the country. How many cars of this size cost as little to keep on the road?

The economy carburettor

Ford have developed a new carburettor with a single variable venturi. In plain English, this automatically adjusts itself to provide the most economical fuel/air mixture whether you're stuck in traffic or cruising on the motorway.

The economy fan

All Cortinas are fitted with viscous coupled fans. When the car is going fast and there is enough air to cool the radiator by itself, the fan disengages. As a fan can consume as much as 5 horse power, this saves petrol and improves performance. The fan also helps the car warm-up faster in the morning, because it doesn't cut in until the engine is hot.

How many cars are this well equipped?

The specification of the Cortina Ghia includes: 1 Remote control door mirror. 2 Cut pile carpeting. 3 Rev. counter. 4 Cigar lighter. 5 3-speed heater fan. 6 Illuminated heater controls. 7 Two speed wipers with intermittent wipe and electric wash. 8 Centre console with radio/stereo cassette and quartz clock. 9 See through head restraints with detachable cushions. 10 Durham/crushed velour seat fabric. 11 Front and rear seat arm rests. 12 Tinted glass. 13 Trip recorder.

Keeping rust from the body

First the whole body shell is washed in an alkali solution and coated with zinc phosphate. Then it's totally immersed in anti-corrosive paint, using an electro-coating process to ensure 100% coverage. Then it gets a further coat of primer and three coats of tough enamel paint. All vulnerable areas like box sections and the insides of the doors are injected with wax. The wheel arches and vulnerable underbody areas are treated with chip resistant PVC coating. And the rear silencer is aluminised.

The Cortina is built to last.

Safety is built in

The Cortina protects you in a rigid steel cage, while the bonnet and boot are designed to crumple progressively and absorb the impact in the event of a collision.

Favourable terms

At last supply equals demand. So if you buy a new Cortina before the end of June, your Ford dealer is in a position to give you very favourable terms. Why not drop in and see him and get the full story.

FORD CORTINA

Range and prices. Ford Cortina Ghia. The car illustrated is the Cortina Ghia.

Cavalier vs. Cortina.
Are you driver enough to notice the difference?

On paper, the Cavalier 1600L is convincingly ahead of the Cortina 1.6L.

Cavalier wins on acceleration, top speed, overall fuel economy, turning circle and boot size.

But on the road, Cavalier beats Cortina even more convincingly. And it's on the road that you, as a driver, will really appreciate the difference.

Cavalier's handling has received constant praise from Britain's leading motor journals.

CAR MAGAZINE, for example, lists Cavalier in their 'Interesting Saloons' category and goes on to rate the handling as 'superb'. Cortina appears in their 'Boring Saloons' class.

Let's look at some other opinions on Cavalier.

WHAT CAR. "Handling is perhaps the best one can get for this class of car, and the steering is light and responsive."

MOTOR. "Offers precise, taut handling, excellent roadholding and is particularly easy to drive."

AUTOCAR. "The Cavalier has the best overall handling and steering by quite a long way; its road-manners are very good indeed."

And in a recent test Autocar again stated "The most satisfactory all rounder of these six cars" (Colt Lancer 1600 GSR, Fiat 131 Supermirafiori, Cortina 1600 GL, Marina 1700 HL, Sunbeam 1600 GLS) "is certainly the Cavalier."

THE TIMES. And a final word from Peter Waymark, the Motoring Correspondent of that distinguished daily newspaper.

Talking of Cortina he says "Nor does the suspension provide the sort of taut handling that distinguishes one of the Cortina's chief rivals, the Vauxhall Cavalier. Although safe enough in most conditions, the car tends to wallow on corners and can be jogged off line by rutted surfaces. The steering is not quite as light and responsive as one would wish and the brakes, though effective, require a good deal of pressure."

CAVALIER 1600L

CORTINA 1·6L

In its class, Cortina has long been one of Britain's favourite cars. But all things must change.

And Cavalier can prove its superiority on practically every count.

Back to the figures on paper. All figures are for the 1600L Cavalier and the 1.6L Cortina.

The Cavalier's top speed of 101 mph beats Cortina by 8 mph. Cavalier's acceleration to 60 mph in 12.3 seconds is over half a second quicker. At 56 mph, Cavalier's 42.2 mpg is 2.4 mpg better.

Cavalier's turning circle, at 31.1 ft. is tighter than Cortina's, and Cavalier's boot at 13.4 cu. ft. is 1.6 cu. ft. bigger.

And price? Cavalier: £4201. Cortina: £4320.

Now back to the road.

Don't you think that as a driver you owe it to yourself to see if you'll appreciate the difference?

Have a chat with your Vauxhall dealer. He'll be in your Yellow Pages.

VAUXHALL 🔷Ⅲ
CAVALIER

UNIT 3: Planning

This unit contains two sections. 'Planning' is nine pages long and has two activities and one assignment. This is the assignment for this unit. 'Being knowledgeable and thinking straight' has one activity and is five pages long. Try to complete this unit in two weeks and set yourself a deadline to get the assignment in to your tutor.

PLANNING

If you look back to Unit 1 you will see that people just starting to study, and people who have been studying for a while, are both fairly preoccupied with *planning* their studies and getting themselves organised.

ACTIVITY 12

Go back to Unit 1 and find and read all the statements by students which are to do with planning. Remind yourself what others say about it.

Many people, probably *most* people, have trouble planning their studies, having a timetable, a schedule or a long-term goal and sticking to it. It isn't just students who have trouble — teachers and university academics do too. They have trouble making priorities between different jobs so that the important ones get done on time. I think this is a perpetual problem for a lot of people, and it isn't one which goes away very easily. But at the same time I don't think it is anything specifically to do with studying, learning or teaching. Like most aspects of studying, I think it is very similar to things we do in other aspects of our lives. The easiest way to get organised in your studying is to see how you manage to get organised in something else, and see how you manage that. However scatty and disorganised you think you are, you are probably quite regular or organised in *something*, whether it's your shopping, planning your holiday, paying your bills, or whatever.

Unit 6, the last in this short course, is called 'Getting organised, getting down to it, and sticking at it'. It looks at how to organise your *studies*. This part of Unit 3 will look at how one organises an *everyday activity*: growing vegetables! I think gardening is a very good analogy for studying in many ways, and it is a particularly illuminating analogy for planning your studies. What I will do here is to discuss what is involved in organising yourself for growing vegetables. This *isn't* in order to teach you about vegetable growing! Rather, I'll be drawing out some general principles which are involved in any sort of planning. These general principles sound a bit trite and obvious on their own, but by seeing what they mean *in practice* I hope they will seem more convincing and useful.

Organising yourself for growing vegetables

I shall probably spend half an hour in my vegetable garden this evening. I do *something*, even if it's only to potter around absentmindedly, almost every evening. What should I do this evening? It's early June and it's warm and humid.

Well, I could just amble around and see what catches my eye. There will be plenty of weeds to dig up or hoe. The runner beans may need tying up. The strawberries may need their suckers removed. These are all routine tasks of maintenance. I don't really need to think about them in advance or plan for them. Provided I just look at the vegetable garden often enough and put in a little time on a regular basis, then these things won't get out of hand and I'll be all right.

There are some things I'm going to have to think about a little and *anticipate*. While the potatoes don't need earthing up just at the moment, soon there will be rather more foliage and earthing up without damaging the stems will become very difficult. So I'd better do that soon. The ground is a bit wet and sticky so I'll leave that until it's a bit drier. I'm also worried about the broad beans. They've grown very tall and top heavy in the wet weather and haven't had to stand up to a high wind since they were small. If there's a gale now it will flatten the lot. I'd better put some canes at the end of the rows and tie string between them to give a little bit of support. I'll write 'bamboo canes for beans' and 'string' on my current shopping list.

A good deal more foresight and organisation is needed for other tasks. I'm worried about my early potatoes at the moment and it's going to cause me problems later on. I was hoping to plant leeks or cabbages where I'd lifted the first rows of early potatoes — but while my leek and cabbage seedlings are ready to transplant, my early potatoes aren't *nearly* ready to lift and eat. Before I work out what to do about this I'd better make sure it doesn't happen *next* year. So I look up what sort of early potatoes I'm using and look in my garden diary to see when I planted them. Well it looks as though I did what I was supposed to, but my notes say the shoots on the potatoes weren't very well developed when I planted them. So next year I must either buy my seed potatoes earlier in order to bring on the shoots more before I plant them, or buy a variety which crops earlier. I ought to write this down in my seed catalogue and start a new list of 'plans' for next year — otherwise I'll forget this.

But what am I to do with my leeks and cabbages *now*? I've got a plan of my vegetable garden with dates for when each patch will be finished with, so I'll consult this. The first patch which will be clear is where the first rows of onions are — but that won't be until September. If I transplant them they'll be rather large, and a bit stunted from being overcrowded in their seed bed. What is more they are the wrong variety to be cut over the next winter. They are supposed to be cut during the late summer.

I have only one alternative. I'll have to use the patch reserved for the tomatoes and forget tomatoes for this year. But that presents me with *another* problem. Vegetables grow best if they are rotated – that is if you change the sort of vegetable which you grow on a particular plot each year. If you grow the same thing in the same place year after year it doesn't grow very well. Last year I grew cabbages where the tomatoes were going to go. So I'll be growing cabbage in the same place two years running. Oh well, it can't be helped. I'll just get a poor crop of cabbages. I'll transplant them there tonight.

I could go on and on like this describing how I decide what to do in my garden. As you can see, while I may be reasonably well organised over the short term, my long-term planning is a bit awry. I seem to be able to spot things coming a few weeks ahead, but I'm not very good at anticipating how the garden will be a few months ahead. One of the reasons for this is, I think, that the garden is simply too complex to keep all the various considerations in mind at one time. How much space things need, how much water, what grows best next to what, what varieties are best, when to plant things and how to rotate crops – it's all too much to think about. I have a couple of diagrams which help a bit in a book which I refer to. One lists all vegetables and has a calendar alongside like this:

	Jan	Feb	Mar	Apr	May	Jun	Jul	Aug	Sep	Oct	Nov	Dec
Artichoke – Globe Perennial. Transplant April							———	———				
Beans – Broad					———	———						
Beans – French						———	———	———				
Beetroot					———	———	———	———				
and so on.												

My seed catalogue has tables of the variations in sowing and harvesting times between different varieties of each type of vegetable. Another of my gardening books has plans of how to lay out gardens and rotate crops. Yet another book is full of scientific evidence about the optimum distances between plants for maximum yields of vegetables – these distances are different from what it says on the seed packets themselves. It's all very complicated, and I haven't worked out a way of combining all this information in a form which enables me to bear everything in mind when I'm planning. I keep a diary and have a plan of how my vegetable plot is laid out. But that doesn't seem to be enough to avoid disasters such as my early potatoes not being ready early! I tend to blunder from one crisis to the next; although the garden isn't *total* chaos, it simply isn't as planned as it could be.

A second reason for my problem is, I think, my lack of flexibility. I simply haven't enough space left over in my garden. It isn't a very big garden and I tend to fill it to overflowing, but this means that when things don't work out as planned, I don't have any room to solve the problem.

I've tried a couple of things to help me plan the garden because I used to be even less organised than I am now. The first thing I tried was regularly watching a gardening programme on television. This was disastrous! The programmes always showed immaculately-kept successful gardens, quite unlike my own. The camera would zoom in on a magnificent cauliflower and the presenter would say, 'This cauliflower is as good as this because I dug plenty of compost into the ground last Autumn, and because I watered the seedlings regularly throughout their growth'. My own cauliflowers were dried up and sitting in soil which had not been composted. In fact I hadn't even got any compost. The programme kept telling me about things I should have done two weeks ago, six months ago or last year, but which were much too late to do anything about now. This was rather like being told once, while I was revising for an exam, that if I'd been revising throughout the course I wouldn't have any trouble! As I hadn't been revising throughout the course this advice wasn't much help to me!

Instead I found a book which told me what to do each month. It says things like: 'Next month you'll need to plant your French Beans, so prepare the ground now'. It has helped me to *anticipate* events and keep on schedule, instead of forever being behind and having missed out crucial steps.

But above all I've got used to simply thinking ahead. This is sometimes evident in the way I choose priorities. For example, it would be nice to get rid of some weeds — they are what I first see when I look at the garden. But I know that unless I get some netting over the strawberries soon they'll start ripening and attracting the birds and I'll lose them all. I've got to buy some netting and probably put an hour or so aside to putting it up, so I'd better get that under way *now* if I want it done by a week from now. So I'd better leave the weeds for the time being. If your studying is at all complex and demanding you will have to make similar choices all the time about what you do and when, and what must be put aside for the time being or even left out altogether. You will have to *plan* your studies.

Let's look back at how I decide what to do in my garden and how I plan this, and see how this is similar to planning your studies. One way of going about studying is to simply sit down, when you have some time, and open your books where you left off last time and carry on with whatever appears to need doing next. I think this is rather like my wandering round my garden, seeing some weeds and getting on with weeding them. I feel as though I'm making progress and getting on with my gardening, but if this is all I do I'm going to get into trouble pretty quickly. And if you don't pay any attention to how you are going to get your next assignment done, or how you are going to finish your course by a certain date, and instead simply concentrate on the particular task in front of you, then you too may run into trouble and get behind. You may need to have medium and long-term plans and be aware of what is coming next.

A second similarity between my gardening and your studying is, I think, in how useful it is to be *flexible*. I tend not to give myself enough *space* left over to cope with things not running to schedule. If I'd had a spare bit of space I could plant my cabbages out without losing my tomatoes. Similarly some students tend not to allow themselves spare *time*. Their timetables for a week's study, or their longer-term plans for how to get units done over a number of weeks, do not have any gaps in them. If they are ill, have a rush on at work, go on holiday or even simply find a particular piece of studying too difficult or boring to finish, then their whole schedule is thrown out of joint. About one week in four or five left completely empty of plans for studying, and an hour or two deliberately left empty in a week's timetable can be enough to prevent this happening. You may need to plan for things going wrong! Even though I don't have as much space in my garden as I would like, I should leave more of it empty to allow me more flexibility. If I decide it's going to take me four working days to write a report, then I should allow myself five. If you've allowed yourself a fortnight for each of the units in this course, allow yourself an extra fortnight overall in order to take into account unforeseen problems which will hold you up, like your tutor going on holiday.

A third similarity is that there is usually quite a lot of information around to help you to plan. I can look in my gardening books to see when things should be done, and I know from experience how long particular tasks take me. In this course there is an estimate of how long each unit will take you, and you know how many units there are. You will also know, from your own experience, how long it took you to do Unit 1, including its activities and assignment.

ACTIVITY 13
Look ahead to Units 4 and 5 and on the basis of how long Units 1 and 2 have taken you (bearing in mind their activities, assignments and how long the units were) estimate how long they will take you:

Unit 4 ......hours

Unit 5 ......hours

It is obviously important that your estimates are reasonably accurate *if your planning* is to work!

A fourth similarity between my gardening and your studying is that I have to choose *priorities* in my gardening. I haven't got enough time or energy to do *everything* so I have to choose between different jobs that need doing. While it is quite easy and satisfying to do the weeding, that isn't the most important thing to do just now. On *this* course you won't have much difficulty with priorities. You can do it *all* without much trouble. But if you were studying with the Open University, for example, you would almost certainly be asked to do rather more than you could possibly do. You'd have to decide whether to read further into a subject that interested you and miss out another topic, or cover everything, but rather superficially. In mathematics and science you'd have to choose between doing plenty of examples of particular problems, or getting rather less experience working with a wider variety of problems, and so on.

A fifth similarity is that it is very useful to use charts, diagrams or lists to help you organise yourself. I use planting and sowing charts, a plan of the layout of my vegetable plot, and lists of notes about what to do next (including a shopping list, for example). In organising your studying you can usefully use exactly the same sort of device. Some people write themselves out a detailed timetable for how they spend every hour of the day. There is an example of one such timetable on page 74. Some people work out long-term schedules so they can see how many weeks or months they have got to complete the units of their course or courses in time for exams or some other deadline. They draw up such schedules as charts so that they can see at a glance whether they are up to schedule and what they've got to do next. This sort of device is described in more detail in Unit 6. It is enough here to recognise that such devices for organising yourself are not specific to studying, but instead are just like the ones we use in all sorts of everyday activities — although we may not be aware that we are using such devices. I think it helps to recognise what you can already do, and to see that you can use the same methods in your studying.

One final similarity I'd like to point out, and one that is perhaps more important than all the others, is that I have rather unrealistic expectations about my garden. Gardening programmes on television show such immaculate gardens and my seed packets have pictures of huge prize-winning vegetables on them. I suppose I want a garden like the ones on television and vegetables like the ones on the seed packets. When things don't match up to these ideals and my planning goes haywire, I sometimes lose sight of how much I *have* managed. My freezer is, after all, still half-full of vegetables from my garden. Similarly, I think students sometimes set their sights too high and have plans for their studies — timetables and schedules — which, while they would be fantastic to keep to are not very realistic. On page nine I quoted a student giving the advice: 'Don't try to do too much. Starting with five hours study a week and building up to ten is better than starting with fifteen and collapsing in a heap'. I think that recognising that even rather moderate goals can be difficult to achieve at first is an important part of planning. The way I organise my garden at present would have been quite impossible a couple of years ago when I started gardening for the first time, and had I planned to achieve what I can now, I would almost certainly have failed.

ASSIGNMENT D
I'd like you to think about an aspect of your own life in which you have needed to organise yourself to some extent to get something done. It could be decor-

ating part of your house, arranging a holiday, organising a dinner party, your hobby, or even arranging your everyday shopping to meet your household's needs. Try and think of anything you do as part of this activity which is to do with *planning*. Start off by just writing down these *planning* parts of the activity. Then try and write about how and why you do this — in what way it helps you — and perhaps in what way you could have been *more* organised about it and planned it more efficiently.

This may seem a rather difficult task and rather hard to get going on. So I've got an example here of how a student tackled this assignment, and also of what the student's tutor wrote in response. This is the letter which the student sent with her assignment:

14 St Aidan's Close,
Leamington Spa,
Warwickshire.
May 5th 1980

Dear Mr Skinner,
    I've enclosed my assignment for Unit 3 — it's the one about organising yourself. I couldn't think of any way in which I was organised — I'm not a very organised person. But my husband reminded me that I'd got the back bedroom decorated before Easter, and that I'd got that done in a fortnight without any major problems so I *must* have been organised! Once I sat down and thought about what I actually did I realised I'd planned it all in my head and done lots of things in preparation for getting the room done.
    I've enclosed the notes I scribbled down as well as my explanation of how I organised getting the room decorated. I hope it makes sense to you!

Yours sincerely,
Betty Williams

This is Betty's assignment:

Assignment for Unit 3

How I organised myself to recorate our back room

Notes
Get room cleared
Strip old paint and paper — buy Polystrippa
Choose paper and paint — get colour cards and catalogues
Buy paper and paint + brushes and paste
(Use kitchen table as pasting table)
(Use kitchen scissors as paper scissors)
Order in room: ceiling, walls, woodwork, paper
Order of paper: *away* from window

There were really three different parts to organising things to get the back bedroom decorated: making sure I'd got the right materials and tools when I needed them; doing the actual decorating in the right order; and making a few domestic arrangements!

I didn't make a list of what I needed, at least only in my head. I intended to buy everything I needed in only two trips to the shops. The first trip I was going to buy things like paste, white spirit, brushes and borrow the colour cards and wallpaper catalogues to choose how we wanted to decorate the room. I'd read in a do-it-yourself manual I'd borrowed about the tools you needed and anyway I'd done it before, though a long time ago. The second trip was going to be to buy the paint and paper we'd chosen. We were going to leave the choosing until after I'd stripped the old paper and paint off so we wouldn't be influenced by what it looked like before.

Things didn't work out like that. I hadn't got the right sort of scraper to get the paint off, and had to go and buy one. The paste I bought was the wrong sort for the paper we chose — it was a vinyl one. I already *had* some white sprit which I'd forgotten about. Then the paper wouldn't stick to the wall because I hadn't put that sealing stuff on first, and I tore some paper because of that and had to buy another roll. I didn't measure the room up for the paint, only for the paper, and I misjudged the amount of paint I needed and had to go and buy another litre. Oh yes, and when I'd stripped the walls I found all sorts of holes I had to fill, so I had to go out and buy some Polyfilla. All in all I had to go down to the shops five times, and we ended up choosing the colours *before* I'd stripped the room bare.

Doing the jobs in the right order was easy in comparison. The book was clear about what to do. The only thing that I didn't do as it said was that waiting for the walls to be finished and dry before I *started* on the woodwork. This would have taken too long, so I did the undercoat on the woodwork while the walls were drying, which made a bit of a mess in a few places. I hadn't taken into account how *long* it would take just doing it in the evenings. I'd have got it done much quicker if I'd put the same time in but done half in the morning and half in the evening so things had a chance to dry. And I didn't hang the paper in the order the book said because, with such a big pattern, I'd have wasted so much paper. Next time I'd choose a smaller pattern (or try and worry less about the order)!

The 'domestic arrangements' were the hardest bit. The less said about that the better, but George (my husband) didn't like sitting downstairs in the lounge on his own while I banged away upstairs, and didn't like having his supper later than usual. We had a row or two about that, especially as it was *my* mother who was coming to stay over Easter. I'm glad it didn't take me longer than a fortnight.

Next time I decorate a room (and I fancy doing up our own bedroom now) I think I'd do the following things differently:

(i) Work out in advance a bit more carefully what needed to be done or bought before what, and what would be best left for the time being. Hopefully this would result in my not forgetting to buy things and not buying things that turn out not to be useful – and fewer trips to the shops!

(ii) Take longer than two weeks but do it in more intense bursts. I'd decided last time to spend an hour *every* evening. Firstly this didn't leave me time to sort things out between tasks (like between stripping the room and choosing the colours). Secondly, especially with the paper-hanging, by the time I'd got the table set up, the paste mixed and a length of paper measured, it was time to stop. I really needed much longer stretches of work for some tasks – though half an hour of gloss painting is enough in one go for me. Thirdly, I'd like some breaks just because I (and my husband) got fed up with decorating *every* night in order to get it done in time.

(iii) Sort out with George, in advance, an agreed way of going about it all. One way or another he's going to have to help or get used to getting his own supper and spending time alone. He's more likely to get used to one of these things if we talk about it in advance rather than just realise after a few evenings what he's in for. If we couldn't agree on this I think I'd get decorators in next time!

This is the letter Betty's tutor sent back when he returned her assignment:

Dear Mrs Williams,

Thank you for your third assignment. It was the longest piece you've written for me and looked as though it was fairly carefully put together, with half an eye on the assignment instructions all the time.

You seem to have learnt quite a lot about how to organise yourself to decorate your next room! Can you see how what you have learnt will be of use to you in organising yourself to study? Let me make some suggestions. Tell me what you think of them in the letter you attach to your next assignment:

1) Different tasks need different lengths of time. Just as papering needs longer than painting, so assignment writing may need a longer stretch set aside than reading a short section.

2) Some things are difficult to plan for in advance. If you try to anticipate them in too detailed a way you can get into trouble. Buying the paste before you know what paste you'll need for the paper you haven't bought yet might be similar to setting an hour aside for the assignment for Unit 4 without looking ahead to see what it's likely to involve you in doing.

3) Planning things for yourself nearly always involves affecting other people's lives as well. You'll come across this issue again in Unit 5. Committing yourself to study will affect those around you, and they

might not like it!

Perhaps you can think of other ways you can learn from your decorating experience?

I'm going on holiday for three weeks, so please don't get too worried (or cross) if your next assignment takes a long time to get back to you.

Yours sincerely,
Martin Skinner

BEING KNOWLEDGEABLE AND THINKING STRAIGHT

Study Notes
This section is presented a little differently from most of the others in this course. Instead of my offering you activities to do every so often, I have written it as one long uninterrupted piece to simply *read*. You will probably have to cope with reading many such pieces of writing, often much longer, in your studies. Except in specially written *courses* (like this one, other National Extension College courses and Open University courses) most of your reading will be like this. For this section I think you should be trying to understand the main points I am making. If you can:

(i)   *decide what you think these main points are,*
(ii) *make sense of them,* and
(iii) *decide what you think of them,*

then you'll have done all I could hope for. I *haven't* gone about writing this section as I suggested one should in the section entitled: '*Explaining in writing*'. I haven't introduced it properly, I haven't divided it up into sections or said what is going to come next, and I haven't even used headings or a conclusion. While this may be poor writing, it is what you will very often have to cope with. Writers of books are often very poor at explaining themselves! All this is going to make your job of understanding what I'm trying to say in this section that much more difficult. If you have trouble, it's probably my fault!

★   ★   ★   ★   ★   ★

Television debates and discussions often have a very characteristic form. First an interviewer will go out into the street and ask passers-by what their opinions are about the topic of the programme. Then it presents some 'hard facts' about the topic. And finally the camera returns to the studio where a panel of 'experts' is assembled to discuss the topic. For example, supposing the topic of the programme was whether the law on abortion should be changed. First we would hear some people stopped in the street expressing their *opinions*: 'It ought to be stopped, it's murder isn't it!' and 'It's got nothing to do with the law — the woman is the person who must make the decision'. The next stage involves us being shown what a human foetus looks like at various different ages: at six weeks, ten weeks, twenty weeks and so on. We are told what the present abortion law is and how many women seek and have abortions. We are told the *facts*. And then in the studio there is a gynaecologist, an abortion counsellor and perhaps a Member of Parliament and a Church of England Bishop too. Between them they discuss the problem of abortion. But what exactly is it that 'experts' *do* when they discuss? When you have learnt about something, as the gynaecologist has, through systematic study, what is it that you can bring to bear to make sense of specific problems such as abortion? In what way is the knowledgeable gynaecologist better equipped than the man in the street to be on the panel of experts?

Well, the apparently obvious answer is that he *knows* more about abortion, and that he can tell people on the panel and in the studio audience things they didn't *know*. I think this is probably *not* his most important contribution. It is a popular conception of academics and 'knowledgeable' people that their main ability is that they can pour forth a torrent of facts. This sort of impression is emphasised by television quiz shows like *University Challenge* and *Mastermind* in which the contestants' *memories* are tested. But remembering isolated facts is only a small and relatively unimportant part of what an academic (or our gynaecologist) can bring to a discussion. More importantly they weigh up the evidence, try to separate facts from opinions, examine arguments for their soundness and generally take a somewhat detached and logical view of things. To some extent, how well our gynaecologist will be able to do these things will depend on how well developed his *ideas* are about the topic, but most importantly it will depend on how well he can *think* and analyse problems. In fact the very word *knowledge* does not mean static isolated *facts* (of the sort tested in *Mastermind*). The word *knowledge* comes from the Greek *gnotos* which means 'known', and the ancient Scandinavian *Lech* which means 'to play' or 'to have sport with'. And so a knowledgeable person is someone who *can play with what is known, and have sport with ideas*, and *not* someone who merely *has facts*.

Very often teachers in universities will say that the subject matter they are teaching is not as important as teaching students to think. When a psychology student leaves university, for example, the specific subject matter of psychology which has been taught to him will not, in most jobs, be nearly as useful to him as the *way of approaching problems* which has been learnt. This should be one of your main goals in studying as an adult. It distinguishes what you are doing now from what you did at school when you were mainly concerned to memorise facts.

But what does this 'way of approaching problems', this 'playing with ideas' and 'thinking' actually consist of? Is it a completely new area which you know nothing about, and which you will have to start learning about from scratch? I think not. As I have emphasised with other aspects of studying, what is involved is very similar to things you are already familiar with in other aspects of your life. I'd like to illustrate this by looking at how one goes about mending a motorbike! This illustration I've borrowed from a book written by Robert Pirsig called *Zen and the Art of Motorcycle Maintenance*. At one point in the book he is trying to explain what logical thinking and scientific method consist of in terms of how he thinks about, and comes to solve, his problems of motorcycle maintenance. You won't need to know anything about motorbikes to make sense of this explanation! Pirsig explains:

> Two kinds of logic are used, inductive and deductive. Inductive inferences start with observations and arrive at general conclusions. For example, if the cycle goes over a bump and the engine misfires, and then goes over another bump and the engine misfires, and then goes over another bump and the engine misfires, and then goes over a long smooth stretch of road and there is no misfiring, and then goes over a fourth bump and the engine misfires again, one can logically conclude that the misfiring is caused by the bumps. That is induction: reasoning from particular experiences to general truths . (p. 99)

In contrast *deductive* inferences do the opposite. They start with general knowledge — what you already know about something — and *predict* that particular things will happen. If I know from my motorcycle handbook and the wiring diagram in it that the hooter is powered by the battery, then I can logically infer, by *deductive inference*, that if the battery is flat, then the hooter won't work.

Now it's not important that you know what inductive and deductive inferences are. What *is* important is that you can recognise that what makes up logical thinking is the same as what makes up some of your everyday thinking. I am not trying to tell you that you are already an accomplished logical thinker. You will need to learn to *apply* what you can do in everyday thinking to your studying. The more complicated and removed from your existing experience is the subject you are studying, the harder it will be for you to apply your everyday thinking. You already use inductive and deductive inferences, but you will have trouble using them deliberately in the context of unfamiliar new subject matter. But logical thinking is not something completely new to you.

Similarly *scientific method* is not something amazingly complex that only incredibly clever scientists can understand and use. You use scientific method all the time. There is even a theory in psychology about how people learn which describes people as being like scientists in the way they deal with the everyday world, and describes learning as a process of carrying out scientific experiments. Let me illustrate what this theory looks like in practice.

I'd like you to imagine that you are walking towards a door which you need to open in order to get into a corridor on the other side. You don't know whether the door opens towards you or away from you. I am now going to describe how you actually get through this door using an everyday description, and also a 'scientific' description. I hope this will illustrate to you that underlying even the most mundane everyday act are quite complex forms of thinking and reasoning. The everyday description is on the left of the page, and the scientific description on the right.

Everyday description	*Scientific description*
1 How am I going to get through this door? Should I push or pull?	Problem: Does the door open inwards or outwards?
2 Well, you can normally tell from the sort of handle on the door	By *inductive inferences* from past experiences I have developed a *theory* about which way doors open, based on the nature of the door handle
3 If I can grab hold of the handle then I'll be able to pull the door, if it's a flat handle then I'll be able to push it	This *theory* states that: i) doors which should be pulled have handles and can be grabbed; and ii) doors which should be pushed have flat handles or plates
4 This door has a sort of large flat plate and nothing I can grab hold of. Normally if you push this sort of door, it ought to open	On the basis of my theory, by deductive inference, I can formulate the *hypothesis* that a door without a grab handle will open outwards if you push it
5 I'll try pushing it	I will carry out a scientific experiment to test my theory about door handles. I will push the door and see what happens
6 It really ought to open	My experimental hypothesis is that when I push the door it will open
7 There, I've pushed the door	I have carried out the experiment
8 The door has opened	The observed result of my experiment is that the door has opened
9 I thought it would!	The experimental hypothesis is confirmed by the experiment
10 I reckon I was right about the handle	My theory concerning door handles has received further support
11 I'll probably be able to work out how to open the next door in the same way	My theory will provide me with a basis for carrying out further experiments with doors

Without being aware of it we are continuously developing our theories about the way the world is, by undertaking such experiments. Sometimes we go about scientific experiments in a rather more conscious and deliberate way. Let's go back to mending a motorcycle. Supposing I couldn't get my motorcycle started. My problem would be 'What's wrong with my bike?' I could *hypothesise* that the problem is that the battery is flat. I could then design an *experiment* to test my hypothesis: I could honk the horn. If it didn't honk then my hypothesis would be confirmed, and the battery would probably be flat, and I might have found the cause of my problem. The actual experiment, the honking of the horn, is only a part of scientific method. Most of scientific method consists of formulating an appropriate hypothesis from a theory, designing the experiment to test the hypothesis, and drawing the correct conclusion from the result. Pirsig has pointed out that people tend to think of the experiment itself as the *whole* of science:

> 'They see lots of test tubes and bizarre equipment and people running around making discoveries. They do not see the experiment as part of a larger intellectual process. . . . A man doing a gee-whiz science show with fifty thousand dollars of Frankenstein equipment is not doing anything scientific if he knows beforehand what the results of his efforts are going to be. A motorcycle mechanic, on the other hand, who honks the horn to see if the battery works is informally conducting a true scientific experiment'. (pp. 101-102)

Asking the right questions, collecting the right evidence or facts and drawing the correct conclusions from these facts – that's what science consists of.

But what has all this to do with the television debate on abortion? Well, if you remember I asked in what way the knowledgeable gynaecologist was better equipped than the man in the street to be on the panel of experts. I said that simply knowing the facts wasn't enough. While the issue of abortion can't be tackled in quite the same rigorous scientific way that working out what's wrong with your motorbike can, the underlying way of thinking about it is very much the same. The gynaecologist will first formulate the question being asked in a manageable way. Instead of 'Is abortion bad?' he'll ask something more specific like 'Is abortion bad for the health of the woman?' and will need to ask an even more carefully formulated question like: 'Does an abortion result in more problems during a woman's next pregnancy?' before he can make any progress. Then he'll have to formulate specific hypotheses like 'An abortion will result in a greater possibility of natural miscarriage during the woman's next pregnancy' in order to know what specific evidence to look at. His 'experiment' will consist of looking at the number of miscarriages following abortions and comparing this figure with the proportion of miscarriages for women who have not previously had abortions. This comparison of figures will lead him to either accept or reject his hypothesis, and so, being careful not to go beyond what this very specific experiment has told him, to develop his theory about the effects of abortion on the health of women. What may appear to the television audience as merely a 'fact' about abortion, is a consequence of the gynaecologist having thought very carefully. What the main in the street states as opinions, the knowledgeable panel will only consider as *hypotheses*, to be tested by carefully looking at the evidence. Each conclusion reached by members of the panel will have been reached (hopefully!) by this careful process of asking the right questions, looking at the relevant facts and drawing the logical conclusions. Even the Bishop will have arrived at his conclusions through the same overall process, though his evidence would be Christian teachings. The man in the street's opinions, on the other hand, are probably ill-informed, muddled, and based on perhaps unsupported assertions made by a newspaper, rather than on sound thinking. The same man in the street may go about mending his car in a thoroughly organised and scientific way, but simply not bring this sort of thinking to bear on issues such as abortion. Obviously it will take this man some considerable practice and care to be able to be knowledgeable about abortion, and to think straight about it, but the basis for this is already there within him; it is not something he has to learn from scratch.

ACTIVITY 14

Now try to answer the following question — go back and re-read part or all of the previous section if you have trouble doing this. Feel free to ask someone else to read it and see what *they* think I'm trying to say.

What do you think were the main points I was trying to make? Try to list perhaps three or four, and very briefly explain what *you* understand them to mean.

I think there is plenty of scope for disagreeing about what the main points of this section were. I have a fairly clear view about what *I* think the most important thing I was trying to say was. It is this:

'What underlies being knowledgeable and thinking straight is not something esoteric and exclusively academic which you have to learn from scratch — you already have the basis for thinking straight within you and you use it all the time in your everyday life.'

There are also a couple of additional points I like to think were important:

'Being knowledgeable does not consist merely of having facts, but of being able to manipulate and "play" with facts in order to use them'

and

'Even scientific method is a straightforward way of thinking which can be seen in simple everyday behaviour'.

I think that almost everything else I said was an elaboration of these points. I used examples and illustrations, sometimes painting quite a vivid picture in order to make my points, but these examples were not important to me in themselves.

Did the points you wrote down include any of mine? There can be no *one* correct interpretation of a piece of writing, so there is room for us to disagree about what the most important points were without this meaning that you have misunderstood me.

I asked a friend to read this section and to write down what she thought were the main points. This is what she wrote:

1. 'Sound thinking is based on scientific method and the link between fact and deduction, and between observation and theory

2. This method of enquiry is not absolutely different from everyday thinking and everyone has experience of using it to deal with the everyday problems of daily life

3. This form of thinking, used consciously on a problem, distinguishes an 'expert' from the man in the street. But it is a difference of *approach* to problems rather than a difference in how much is *known*.

4. A knowledgeable man is therefore one who "has sport with ideas" rather than one who has a good memory.'

UNIT 4: Remembering

This unit is about how you remember things. It's in four parts:

1 *Your memory is bigger and better than you thought!*
2 *Your memory is not like a tape-recorder.*
3 *Memory over long periods works differently from memory over very short periods.*
4 *Remembering things involves actively reconstructing them.*

Deliberately memorising things isn't a crucial part of learning. Knowledgeable people look things up in books all the time rather than trying to remember everything. But nevertheless it is helpful to understand a little about how your memory works, so that you can control it better, and so that you can remember things in exams should you ever need to.

Unlike Units 2 and 3 this unit only has one section. It has *nine* activities which will involve you in, among other things, reviewing the course so far. There is no assignment for this unit. I suggest you try and complete this unit in · *one* week.

1 Your memory is bigger and better than you thought!

What did you have for supper yesterday? Can you remember in detail what it was? And how about details of where you were sitting? What happened during supper? Can you remember what you talked about or thought about?

ACTIVITY 15

Write down everything you can remember about supper last night, just as it occurs to you, in any order. Only stop when you lose interest in doing this!

Most people can get back to these sorts of memories, with a little nudging and a few clues, so as to be able to recall the most extraordinary trivial details, sometimes with some vividness. With a little more help most people can even recall details of what they were doing, say, exactly a year ago. The surprising thing is that you did not *deliberately memorise* what you had for supper yesterday, but you can nevertheless remember it. In fact the vast proportion of our memory seems to work quite automatically and effortlessly. But this is absurd, you might say. You surely can't remember *everything!* There wouldn't be enough room in our memories! But it is now recognised that our memories are effectively infinitely large − that there is *no limit* to the quantity of information we can store away. It is also generally believed by psychologists that memories do not simply 'fade away' over time, but that our failure to recall things is due to problems we have in *finding* or *reconstructing* our memories when we need them. In other words our memories store a record of a very great deal of everything we do, and *keep* this record stored away for future use.

Why is it, then, that if we store everything away and our memories stay there, largely intact, that we have such difficulty in remembering specific things? Well, it's because we can't *find* our memories. Our memory is so vast and complicated, like a huge library, that it is terribly difficult to *find* what we want. 'But if you can't find it, how do you know it's really there?', you may ask! Well we know it's there because we can recognise things which we can't remember. For example I'm sure you've often forgotten someone's name, but when you are reminded of it, you immediately *recognise* it. You *knew* the name all along, and you had it stored away in your memory, but you simply couldn't *find* it. This process, of 'looking for' memories, you have probably often used deliberately. If you've left your front door key somewhere round the house and you can't remember where it is, you may have, in your imagination, re-traced your steps to where you last had the key, or thought of the likely places you would have put it down. What you are doing is recalling similar, or likely memories, and seeing whether you recognise part of them as what actually happened. However, normally this 'search' for the memory you've lost is an unconscious activity − it works very quickly, efficiently and *effortlessly*.

As you get older, and have more experience in the world, so you have accumulated more memories. If you find it harder to remember things than you used to, this is *not* because your memory is somehow full up, or that as you get older memories fade away faster. It is also probably *not* that the process of storing away memories has somehow got rusty. What is probably happening is that you have very many more memories to search amongst to find the ones you want! What is more, many of your memories will be rather similar, and it will be difficult to tell them apart. Supper last night might have been such an ordinary everyday supper that you can't easily distinguish it from the hundreds of similar suppers you've had over the last few years. The problem is not that you have no record of last night's supper, but that you can't distinguish it from other records. It might simply have been recorded as: 'Same old fish and chips supper while watching the news on TV. The tea was cold, as usual'. How *distinctive* memories are is one important factor which determines whether you can remember them or not.

2   Your memory is not like a tape-recorder

It sometimes seems as though your memory simply makes an exact record of what you saw or heard, rather like a film or tape-recording. You can probably 'picture' people's faces in your mind, and your memory of last night's supper may well involve 'pictures' and maybe even the sound of someone speaking to you. You can also probably 'hear' a favourite piece of music when you remember it. However, memory does not work very well in this rather literal 'photographic' way. Usually such 'pictures' and 'echoes' are rather incomplete and shadowy and often rather inaccurate. What memory usually does is to *reconstruct* what you originally experienced. This reconstruction will mean much the same, but will differ in many details. Let me give an example:

ACTIVITY 16

Without turning back to the beginning of this section, what questions did I ask you about last night's supper? Try and recall them as accurately as possible.

OK. You can now look back and check whether you were correct.

What you almost certainly found is that you remembered roughly what the questions were about, but *not* the exact form of words. What you stored in your memory was not the questions as I wrote them and you saw them, but the *sense* you made of them – what they *meant* to you. The sense you made of these questions will have been added to, and changed, by reading other parts of this section in which I referred to these questions or to your memory of last night's supper. All these additions will have helped you, without any effort, to 'reconstruct' the original questions. In fact it is very hard work persuading your memory to do anything else than store what something means to you. If something doesn't make sense, it is *extremely* difficult to store and recall it at all.

I'll give a few little examples of how this works. I'd like you to read this list of letters through once, quite quickly, and then shut your eyes, count to twenty, and then, keeping your eyes shut, try and remember them

YBIF – AGFREBA

How did you do? Most people would have trouble remembering more than a couple (in the correct order) after ten seconds. Now do the same thing with these letters. Read through them once, quickly, and then count to twenty before trying to recall them:

BABY – GIRAFFE

Too easy, wasn't it?! But they were exactly the same letters!

The same thing happens with words. Try the same task with:

gossip secrets is jurymen about by halted trial

– which is very hard, whereas:

— is much easier. Something you might have done when reading the first of these two 'sentences' (if you were cheating) was to try and somehow make some sense of it. You may have noticed that some of the words were closely related (e.g. *trial* and *jurymen*) and even have formed a phrase, by linking backwards and forwards through the words (e.g. 'jurymen gossip about secrets!). Any such efforts at *organising* or *making sense* of the words would have greatly helped you when you came to recalling the words (though they may have resulted in your getting the *order* wrong!). Another way you might have cheated is to have read through the first 'sentence' several times, repeating it to yourself. Such repetition is hopelessly ineffective. I remember as a child being sent to the local shop to buy some tomato sauce. I repeated 'tomato sauce, tomato sauce. . .' to myself all the way to the shop, and when I was asked by the shopkeeper what I wanted I had forgotten! I had to go all the way home again to ask my mother. People are so hopelessly bad at *deliberately* memorising things that almost *any* task which focuses on the *meaning* of what is to be memorised works better.

ACTIVITY 17
To illustrate this, I'd like you to go through the following list of animals making a decision about each animal: is each a bird, a reptile, or a mammal? Give your answer by ticking the correct box on the right. Do this as quickly as you can.

	Bird	*Reptile*	*Mammal*
Adder ·······			
Thrush ·······			
Heron ·······			
Crocodile ······			
Elephant·······			
Vulture ······			
Alligator ······			
Magpie ······			
Cow ········			
Mouse ········			
Penguin ·······			
Rattlesnake ·····			
Chimpanzee ····			
Lizard ········			

Now read on.

Now I'd like you to simply go through this second list as fast as you can just *three times, saying the words out loud.* I'm going to test your memory of this *second* list of words later on in this section.

cauliflower, pansy, grapefruit, banana, potato, parsnip, chrysanthemum, daffodil, beetroot, dahlia, cherry, pineapple, spinach, crocus, peach.

Now read on without looking back over these two word lists. The points I've made above may seem reasonable, you may say, when what you are trying to memorise makes some sense. But some people appear to be able to remember factual information which *doesn't* make sense – a list of random numbers for example. However, even apparently meaningless numbers can sometimes make sense.

I'd like to recount one little incident about memory for numbers which illustrates this point. I was once asked by a friend what sort of car it was ahead of us in a traffic jam. I immediately answered, 'Oh, a Volvo 245 or 265 I think'. 'Good heavens!', my friend exclaimed, 'however can you remember numbers like that?' In fact I hadn't remembered the numbers. I'd *worked them out*. I knew that Volvo car numbers *mean* something. The first number is the *series* of car. This was the latest boxy, square edged car, so I knew it was a series 2. The last number I knew meant the number of doors – it was an estate car with 5 doors. The middle number I knew meant the number of cylinders the engine had. I couldn't tell how many cylinders it had, of course, except that it must be 4 or 6, so I'd identified it as a *245* or *265*. In contrast I *can't* identify Fiat cars. I know they are numbered between about 124 and 136 at the moment, but I've no idea what the numbers *mean* and so I can't say 'Oh, that's a Fiat 128'. I simply don't remember which car has which number, I only remember the 'rules' about what the numbers mean. It is very much easier to remember a rule from which you can work out lots of answers than it is to remember all the answers.

It is nevertheless possible, of course, to remember even complete nonsense if you are willing to put enough effort into it. Telephone numbers are a good example and people use all sorts of little tricks to help their memory. The numbers themselves mean nothing, but by working out the relationships between the numbers or rhyming the numbers with words which are easier to remember, it is often possible to quickly remember new telephone numbers. People who specialise in carrying out these sorts of memory tricks are called *mnemonists* and some can carry out the most phenomenal feats of memory with these tricks, recalling vast amounts of material word for word. If you'd like to try to master some of these tricks you might like to try to find and read one of these books. They are both cheap paperbacks:

The Mind of a Mnemonist, Luria, Penguin
Speed Memory, Tony Buzan, Sphere.

However, mnemonics can be very time-consuming to develop, and very tedious to use.

Luckily, recalling meaningless information word for word isn't at all important in studying. Rather you are involved in remembering *ideas* through *using* them. Even if you *do* find you need to remember a list of information, I think you'll find you already know how to do it!

ACTIVITY 18

Without looking back, write down the *two* lists of words I showed you earlier (Yes, I want you to recall the first list as well, even though I didn't at the time ask you to memorise it!).

List 1	*List 2*

If I'm right, you will have remembered more of List 1 than List 2. You will probably have written down the birds, reptiles and mammals separately — these categories will have helped you break the list up and give you *clues* as to what the animals were. It's much easier to remember three categories than fifteen words. If you remembered many of List 2 then I would guess that you did so by noticing that the words were all vegetables, fruits or flowers, and doing the same sort of classification as for List 1, and recalling the words in the three groups.

The important point is that the simple act of imposing some sort of meaningful structure on the list of words resulted in your remembering some of List 1 *without effort*. The actual process of recalling the words was probably a sort of guided reconstruction — you may have used the categories to suggest which words *might* have been the ones I gave you and then recognised some of them, e.g. 'Well, what sort of reptiles are there? Um . . . snakes are reptiles, let's think . . . python? No! Rattlesnake? Yes! etc. etc.' This is *so* much easier and more efficient than trying to repeat the list of words, by rote, just as you saw them. If you try to imitate a tape-recorder you will not be using the amazing capacity your memory naturally has.

3 Memory over long periods works differently from memory over very short periods

I can remember, as a schoolboy, being required to recite short poems from memory in class. I had to memorise a poem for homework the night before, and I used to spend hours painfully working at this tedious task. Nevertheless I could seldom recite more than a few isolated phrases next day. One of my problems was that I hardly ever understood the poems. Their language, metre and rhyme made no sense to me — my mind was a blank when I read them. As I discussed in the previous sections, you remember what you have made sense of, and I hadn't made much sense of these poems. But I had another problem. I used to read out loud a line of the poem, close my eyes, and then immediately recite it from memory. This wasn't too hard, and it gave me the feeling of knowing the poem. I'd go through the whole poem this way, testing myself *immediately* after having read the line. Unfortunately this strategy was hopeless for remembering even a few hours later.

It is now understood by psychologists that memory for fairly small amounts of information over very short periods (perhaps up to 20 seconds) works in a *very* different way from memory over longer periods. It is reasonably easy to see why this should be so. In order to understand a sentence you read (or one you hear) you need to 'store' the first half of the sentence in your memory until you get to the end, and then make sense of the whole sentence together. (If you had no such very brief memory you wouldn't be able to understand sentences or speech at all!) It seems we have a special device in our heads for doing this, which can hold about half a short sentence in memory for a very short while. When you get to the end of the sentence and have understood it, you no longer need to keep the first half in your memory, so this device throws it out in order to be ready for the next sentence. The half-sentence stored in this little memory device usually does not even get as far as your big main memory but is immediately forgotten, as you saw when you tried to recall the questions I asked you about last night's supper. You didn't remember the questions word for word, but only your understanding of the gist of the questions. As I didn't have any *understanding* of the lines of the poems, I remembered practically *nothing*.

This is important if you are trying to memorise material, as you may be able to repeat it to yourself from memory immediately after reading it, but still not remember anything at a later date. This won't be because you have a terrible memory, but because you are trying to use the wrong sort of memory.

4 Remembering things involves actively reconstructing them

I've used the expression '*reconstructing* memories' a number of times now. What does it mean, in practice? Well when I asked you to remember your supper last night, what you were almost certainly *not* about to do was turn back to six o'clock and start running your memory back like a film recording. We get access to this sort of memory rather patchily and build up a picture rather slowly. Perhaps you remember what you ate first, then something you read in the paper, then that the dog kept wanting to go in and out of the back door, and gradually your recollection fills out. You have reconstructed suppertime from fragments. If you were asked to do this in an exam, to *test* your memory of suppertime, you would have to not simply list things as they occurred to you, but put them together into an account. And in the process of putting them together you would probably remember more and more as one thing cued another. I'd like to demonstrate this sort of process by helping you to reconstruct the first two units of this course *from memory*!

ACTIVITY 19

To start off, I'd like you to simply list the first few things you can remember which were in either of the first two units. Take a couple of minutes and make a short list, perhaps half a dozen items, of whatever occurs to you. Don't look back to check!

When I asked my colleague Alistair to do this, this is what he wrote down:

— about who studies this course
— is Concorde noisy?
— Questionnaire thing
— Notts Forest vs. Liverpool
— Lots of statements by students
— giving directions to Leamington (three times)

ACTIVITY 20

With your own list (and Alistair's) what I'd now like you to do is *organise* it a bit. Which *order* were these items in, and which bits went in which units? Were some items really like headings, and others like sub-headings or detailed bits under a heading? Try *organising* the bits you've remembered. As you do this, you'll probably find it reminds you of other things. Write these down too. Go ahead and try this for *another* couple of minutes.

Again I asked Alistair to do this, and this is what he wrote down:

Unit 1   - about who studies this course
      descriptions of students

      - about what it's like studying
      statements by students
      (lots about being organised)

      - a questionnaire about what I felt about
      starting. I remember feeling anxious

Unit 2   <u>Writing</u> - giving directions to Leamington

          - directing a stranger to my local
          railway station. Not too much
          detail

      <u>Comparing things</u>

          - blokes arguing about Notts
          Forest and Liverpool in a pub

          - two essays on Concorde being noisy:
          One was like a list of facts and
          the other was like an argument

          <u>EVALUATING!</u>

Alistair told me:

'Even as I wrote things down I was remembering more. For example when I wrote the word EVALUATING down I'd just remembered that's what the message was: 'being evaluative', that was it! I could explain more about that now if you like. I'd forgotten that when I first wrote my list'.

I imagine much the same sort of thing happened to you. Now I'd like you to go one stage further.

ACTIVITY 21

This time (and this will be the last time I'll ask you to work on remembering Units 1 and 2) I'd like you to take your list (and Alistair's) and ask a couple more questions about them:

1   Were there any other sections or topics? Have you left any gaps? Try and fill in places where you think you've missed something out.

2   What do your brief notes mean? For a statement like 'giving directions to Leamington' in Alistair's list, what was this made up of? What parts did it have? What was it for? What *details* can you fill in under your headings?

Generally expand your description of what was in Units 1 and 2 in this way. Carry on filling it out until you feel stuck or bored. Allow yourself at least twenty minutes. Just how much *can* you remember?

I hope this process of *reconstructing* your memory of Units 1 and 2 worked for you. Most people find that they can do this by *asking questions* of their memories. If you write out what you *can* remember and use that to help you get access to what you *can't*, then you will usually remember more. You can do this reconstruction very deliberately by asking the sorts of questions I asked you — about the *structure* and *order* of items, about what is *missing* and what *details* you can remember. There are probably many other ways *you* remembered more about Units 1 and 2. Looking back at Alistair's second list, the questions I would ask him to help him remember more would include:

'What sort of students *do* study this course?'
'What are these students' statements about?'
'Was there anything else in Unit 1?'.
and so on.

You can use this process of reconstruction during your learning as well. For example you can use it to see what you missed out in the first place. If you now look back at Units 1 and 2 you will find bits which aren't included in your final list. If you fill in the gaps (and maybe correct yourself where you were a bit hazy) you'll be polishing up your reconstruction.

Next time you try to remember what Units 1 and 2 were about you will be able to reconstruct them more completely. It's partly through recognising what you *can't* remember and *haven't* learnt that you can learn.

ACTIVITY 22

I'd like you to try to remember what the different parts of this section on remembering were called. I'm not interested in the exact wording, only the general meaning of the headings. You probably won't be able to remember them straight away, so try to *reconstruct* the whole section until you've *worked out* what the headings must have been. Then check to see if you were right.

ACTIVITY 23

Now try to remember what Unit 3 was about. Go through the same procedure as Alistair went through to remember Units 1 and 2. Try and write as complete a description as you can before looking back at Unit 3 to check and fill in the gaps.

UNIT 5: How do you learn best?

In Units 2, 3 and 4 we saw how studying involves many abilities which we already use in our everyday activities. But it is not only in our *everyday* activities that we have done things very similar to studying. We have all actually gone about some deliberate learning as well. Firstly, we all have years of school experience behind us. Even if this experience was a very long time ago it probably still plays a significant part in the way we react to teachers now, the way we feel about *having* to learn something, and our sense of being a strong or weak student. The learning you will be doing now will be very different from the sort of learning you did at school, and it is important to recognise some of these differences. Secondly, we all have had learning experiences since we left school. We have learnt how to handle tasks at work, how to cook, mend the car, or grow vegetables successfully. We have learnt some simple First Aid or what to look for when watching football. It obviously isn't necessary to have been taught in order to have learnt something, and many of our learning experiences will be very informal ones – not connected with courses, hard work or exams. Much of this sort of learning is hard to recognise as it may not seem to involve much *studying*.

However, you may have watched a TV series on gardening or cookery and subsequently bought the BBC book of the series and fairly systematically applied some of what you have learnt. You may have gone to St John's Ambulance lessons on First Aid, or evening classes on car maintenance. You may simply have watched your local football team and *Match of the Day* every week, and talked about it with your friends and gone on to read a football coaching manual. All of these seem to me to be rather more like organised studying. It still may not seem like school work, but it is close to what effective independent learning is about. From your experiences of such learning you will already have formed a number of impressions of what seems to work best for you – how you learn best. If I was simply to ask you straight out how you learn best, you'd probably have difficulty in telling me very much. But if you think back to specific occasions when you have been deliberately learning about something you will probably remember some aspects of the learning which were more effective or enjoyable than others. One way of highlighting these aspects is to think back to two very contrasting learning experiences and think about how they differed and why.

This is what this assignment requires you to do.

ASSIGNMENT E: Good and bad learning experiences
Write short accounts of *two* learning experiences you have had. One should be a rather bad experience, where you felt you learnt little or nothing, which you didn't perhaps enjoy, and which makes you feel rather negative about studying. The other should be a much better experience: some learning which you feel was worthwhile, enjoyable, or encouraging. Simply describe the two experiences, pointing out the ways in which they were bad and good. Then try and explain *why* they were different, and what you can do to make your present studying more like your good experience. Try and describe your two experiences in less than 200 words each, and your analysis and conclusions from them in less than another 200 — about 500 or so words in all. Don't worry if you find you have less to say (or indeed can't get it all down in the words!) — simply send off to your tutor whatever you have written. The purpose of this assignment is to help you think about how you can make learning more effective and enjoyable for yourself by noticing what has tended to work for you in the past. The more clearly you describe your experiences, the more easily your tutor will be able to understand and so be able to make suggestions and ask further questions about your learning. If you like you can also write a few comments about any difficulties you had in writing this assignment, and what you think are its strong and weak points. You can put these comments in a letter to your tutor attached to the assignment.

Here is an example of the written work a student submitted for this assignment, together with his tutor's comments. I hope these comments will help you see what your tutor will be looking for and the sorts of ways he will be able to be helpful.

> 74 Chatterton Road.,
> Guildford,
> Surrey,
> Tues. 5th Oct.

Dear Mr Johnson,
    I've enclosed my latest assignment — I'm sorry it is overlength. I couldn't get down to writing to start with, but once I'd tried to explain to my wife what it was I wanted to say it came much easier. In fact as you can see I had difficulty keeping it short. I could have given a much more detailed description of the photography classes, but I suppose it's good to get used to trying to be brief. I'm afraid the third part is a bit muddled. It just sort of flowed in no particular order. Would it help next time if I write the points I want to make down on separate pieces of paper and sort of shuffle them together in a more logical way before I write a final version?

I've got a lot on at work at the moment so I may be a bit slow with my next assignment. I hope that's O.K.

Yours sincerely,
William Woodworth
Student 701842

Mr William Woodworth   *701842*   *Learning to Study*

Tutor: Mr Johnson

Assignment E   *Good and bad learning experiences*

Thinking of a bad experience was easy. Even now, forty years after I left school I can remember my awful French classes. For every lesson we had to learn a list of vocabulary — just twelve or so words and what they were in English. I couldn't even remember half of them. I'd get two out of ten and have to call out my score so everyone would know. The teacher would be sarcastic: *"Two,* eh Woodworth!" I could have died. I used to try and try, just staring at the words and saying them over and over, but nothing ever happened. I wasn't so bad at other subjects, just French.

I suppose it was 'bad' because I didn't learn anything. Nothing. I don't remember more than a few words of French after *three years* of French classes twice a week. It was also horrible — I mean I dreaded classes and felt awful while I was trying to learn the words. It just seemed so hopeless and inevitable that I'd do badly.

Thinking of a good experience was much harder. I've always associated studying with having to do things I don't like, and doing badly. But there *are* things I've enjoyed finding out about, but I suppose I haven't thought of them as studying. A few years ago I got fed up with the 'holiday snaps' I used to take with my pocket camera and decided to get better at it. I didn't know how to choose a decent camera so I went to the library and took out a book on photography. It was a bit technical and off-putting and I told the librarian this and she looked up in a booklet and found an evening class on photography at the local school, and found me a *'Which?'* report on which camera to buy. The first evening at the class I felt a bit of a fraud with my shiny new camera. I thought all the others would be experienced and know about f-stops and film speeds and all those things, but it turned out they were as new to it all as I was. Every week someone would bring in some photos they'd taken and we'd talk about what had gone wrong and the teacher, a young bloke, would make just a few gentle suggestions. He didn't overwhelm us with information. Just when we needed to know something, or someone wanted to try something new, like developing their own film, then he'd give us a bit of a talk. It was amazing because I can still explain all the processes involved in developing film off the top of my head. No effort at all! I didn't miss a single evening class right through that awful winter.

Obviously I *wanted* to learn about photography, whereas I didn't have any choice about being at the French classes. And even though I did *try* to learn the French vocabulary, it was only to pass the tests and avoid being shown up in front of my friends again. I didn't expect I'd ever *use* any of the French words. Now when I've been to France on holiday I feel I'd like to speak French just a little, but I've got a block about it. I couldn't bring myself to go to French evening classes. I think some people aren't cut out to be linguists. I didn't seem to have any trouble remembering all the stuff about photography. I was more interested, and anyway I needed to know it if I was going to produce better photographs to take into the next class. The other thing was that at the photography class they were a really nice bunch of people. I didn't feel a fool asking them questions or admitting I didn't know something, though as I've already said, I was a bit apprehensive at first. When the year was over I went back to the library and that technical book made a lot more sense. I've read quite a lot since then and I've now got my own dark room at home. I've never looked at a French book again though!

ACTIVITY 24

Imagine you are Mr Johnson, the tutor to Mr Woodworth. Write Mr Woodworth a letter in reply to his assignment. What would you want to tell Mr Woodworth about his assignment? Are their any questions you would want to ask him? Be as helpful as you can in encouraging Mr Woodworth to learn from his past experiences of learning. Take up to half-an-hour on this.

This is the letter Mr Johnson actually wrote to Mr Woodworth. How does it compare with your own?

27 Finsbury Park Road,
London, NW.
Thurs. 7th Oct.

Dear Mr Woodworth,

Thank you for your first assignment; I enjoyed reading it.

Explaining to your wife what you intend to write sounds like an excellent way of both getting your thoughts organised and making sure you will be understood. Your idea of shuffling your points around on separate pieces of paper also seems likely to be very helpful. You can jot down ideas, as they occur to you, without worrying about how they fit in, and then concentrate on organising these ideas into a coherent argument when you come to write your assignment. This may also help you write more briefly. Please tell me how this method works out for you.

Yes, it is perfectly all right for you to delay doing your next assignment. Try not to leave it too long or you may lose momentum. More structured courses with a heavier workload may not give you this luxury, so it may be good practice to try to fit your studies in despite being pushed at work.

My comments on your assignment are on an attached sheet. I'll look forward to reading your next piece of work.

Yours sincerely,
Paul Johnson

Good and bad learning experiences

Mr Woodworth

Your descriptions of your learning experiences were very vivid, and gave me a strong impression of what they were like, and a good deal of material to work with. Your conclusions, as you say in your letter, were a bit muddled and you didn't go on to suggest what you can learn from these experiences to make your present learning more efficient and enjoyable. I'd like to suggest a number of possibilities:

(i)   Simply trying to *memorise* lists of apparently meaningless material (French vocabulary) can be a dull, difficult and fruitless task. Trying to *understand* something (how to develop films), especially when you need to understand in order to *do* something, can be much easier, more enjoyable, and can sometimes make memory practically effortless.

(ii)   Being *anxious* about learning (your two out of ten being exposed to the class, and expecting others at the photography class to be experts) can greatly inhibit you and make learning unlikely, or even prevent you from starting.

(iii)   *Discussing* what you are learning (with your photography class, or with your wife) can be invaluable. The social support can be as important as the development of ideas which takes place.

(iv)   *Discovering* things for yourself, following up your own interests, and being actively involved in what you are learning, can make an enormous difference.

(v)   Learning for *yourself* is easier than learning for *others*.

Other points you might have highlighted include:
- being overwhelmed with information is bad
- sympathetic teachers really help

- having some goal in mind (taking better photos) helps
- gentle first steps (evening classes) can lead on to more advanced learning (managing the technical book from the library).

You may well be able to think of several more such points now that I have started listing in this way. Clearly there are a number of things to look out for which will help you in your studying, and which you can learn from your past experiences.

Can you imagine how you might now be able to tackle learning to speak a little French in a more positive way than you did at school? Try and list a few points.

Paul Johnson

ACTIVITY 25

Is this the sort of correspondence you had expected to happen between a student and a tutor? In particular, were there any points which struck you about the manner in which Mr Woodworth wrote, and the manner in which Mr Johnson replied? *Was this how your school teachers marked your essays?* Have another look at Mr Woodworth's letter and assignment, and at Paul Johnson's reply and comments, with these questions in mind and then move on and see what I noticed.

There are two things which occurred to me about Mr Woodworth's assignment. Firstly, as you may have noticed, he has written in a *very* informal way, almost as if he was *talking* to his tutor. This may have been very helpful to him in expressing himself clearly and in getting down to writing his thoughts at all. He certainly seems to have come across very vividly as a result. On the other hand, this level of almost chatty informality may have got in the way of him expressing himself *precisely*. Our spoken arguments tend to be a bit jumbled, but we need to be fairly orderly in the way we make written points if we are to make a coherent argument which leads on to a clear conclusion. In attempting to write more formally, however, you may find ideas harder to express, and you may tend to cover up what you really think and feel.

Secondly, I think Mr Woodworth is being very open. When he is having difficulty, he says so, and if he has a little half-formed idea, he suggests it to his tutor. This gives his tutor much more idea of what sort of a learner Mr Woodworth is, and what sort of comments and suggestions are likely to be helpful. There are no marks on this course, and no prizes to be won. The only reward is improving your studying. So the more you tell your tutor about what seems to be difficult (as well as what you find easy), the more you are likely to get help to improve.

You may find this a bit dangerous — laying yourself open to seeming silly — but most important learning seems to involve taking some risks, and your tutor will be trying to be helpful rather than critical.

You may also have noticed several things about the way the tutor tried to be helpful. He offered a more carefully structured and more thoughtful analysis of Mr Woodworth's assignment. He made several *suggestions*. And he offered a *task* for Mr Woodworth to do: 'Can you imagine how you might now be able to tackle learning to speak a little French. . .?'). He *didn't* give a mark out of ten, say 'Right!' or 'Wrong!' anywhere, or criticise spelling or punctuation.

Your tutor will be making similar attempts to listen carefully to what you have to say and to offer his ideas and suggestions. In addition he or she will be paying attention to how you are tackling this course — how you manage to write the assignments, and whether you are able to work regularly through the course, for example. The more you tell your tutor about this, the more you are likely to be given a thoughtful reaction.

UNIT 6: Getting organised, getting down to it and sticking at it

In Unit 3 you worked through a section on 'Planning'. In it you looked at the way everyday activities are planned, and did an assignment describing how you had organised yourself to do something. In this unit you will have the opportunity to apply some of what you learnt about planning to the organisation of your own studies.

This unit begins with a description of how I struggle to organise myself, and then gives two examples of students' assignments. The students describe how they have organised their studies and their tutor comments on this. There are also two activities and the final assignment of the course in this unit. I suggest you try and complete the unit in one week.

Some of the biggest headaches of studying on your own are to do with:

1   *getting yourself organised:* so that you know what you've got to do, when you've got to get it done by, and how you are going to fit it into a busy life;

2   *getting down to it:* so that when you have got time available for studying you don't instead spend it watching TV, going down to the pub, or staring vacantly over your books at the wall opposite your desk;

3   *sticking at it:* so that once you've started you don't get stopped by the first sentence you can't finish writing, bored after reading two pages, or decide that it's about time you wrote to Auntie Flo.

These aren't headaches which go away easily. I've suffered from all three of them during the writing of this course, and I expect them to always be waiting to hit me whenever I get too sloppy and ill-disciplined in my work. However I have developed, over the years, some ways of keeping these headaches at bay. These are not clever or involved devices, and are certainly not unique. I wouldn't expect anyone else to find exactly the same devices entirely suitable for them, but nevertheless it may be helpful if I briefly describe the main things which seem to help me.

1   Keeping at hand a list of tasks to do

As I realise I need to get something done, like writing to someone, reading an article in order to discuss it with a friend, or phoning a student about some administrative matter, so I write it down on my latest list. When most of the tasks have been done I start a new list by writing down the tasks which I haven't done

69

yet. These tend to be the bigger, and often more important, tasks, which I can't bring myself to get down to. The list reminds me I'm not doing them, and they end up at the top of my list.

TASKS TO DO: 12ᵗʰ JUNE

1) Finish writing chapter for Andy
*2) Tax forms DEADLINE JUNE 14th
3) Letter to Naomi   (i) what i've been doing
                       (ii) permission to take time off
4) Find out how much
   "guides" cost   - get budget code 0028375
                        - Charge Bet Committee
5) Phone Andy about OUP
6) Check Alistair is ok. for Steve's seminar
                       (get seminar dates fixed)
7) Car: - fix radio   *
                       - fix seat belts   (must)
                       - Change tyres ✓
8) Get D304 blocks - Martin Hammersley's bits
                     in Blocks 3+4 on
                     qualitative methodology
9) LIBRARY   (i) Brians article
                       (ii) Order Perry (get from Dai)
                       (iii) anything in factor analysis?
10) Arrange meeting with Dave re thesis
11) Letter to Tony — see Brendan ?? NO!
12) Register baby (Leamington Registrar)
                    9-68227. 2. Euston Square
13) Birthday card to Steve
14) ....

---

2 Keeping a diary

I used to be very haphazard about this, but my life has got too complicated to keep dates in my head or on scraps of paper. I found it quite difficult using my diary regularly at first, but now find it invaluable though I'm still a bit erratic. I can see how long I've got to finish big tasks; I can see when I'm going to be pushed and when things are going to be a bit quieter; it helps me plan when to try to get tasks done by, and whether I've got time to even take jobs on at all. For long-term planning, over the next four months, say, I sometimes make myself a wallchart, so I can see which *weeks* will be hopeless and which I'll be able to sit down in to get lots of reading and writing done. Long-term deadlines, like exams or a committee meeting for which I'm writing a report, make it very clear what has got to be fitted in, and what has got to be left out. I'm too busy to fit *everything* in, but my diary helps me fit the important things in first. I've always wanted to do more than I have the time or energy to do, and without a little bit of planning the gap between my aspirations and harsh reality would be even greater, I think. Now my first baby has arrived I shall probably have to be rather *more* organised. I put social and family commitments in my diary, as well as work commitments.

3 Having somewhere to work

When I shared a flat in London a few years ago I always found it much harder to get down to work than I do now. At present I have the space to leave my books, folders and umpteen pieces of paper out on the table where I work. I can see them lying there waiting for me, and if I sit down I can start work almost immediately. If necessary I can leave for a few minutes (to answer the phone) or hours (to go shopping) and come back and carry on exactly where I left off. No one needs the table space, and it doesn't need to be tidy for others, so I can simply put my pen down and leave, knowing nothing will be disturbed. Also I know I won't be disturbed too much if I'm working at my table. In contrast in my flat in London it was quite a business setting myself up for work. I had to wait until people were out of the way, clear a space, collect my things together and lay them out around me. If I needed to stop, even for a short while, I had to put everything away again. Little wonder that I didn't get down to work as easily, or as often, as I do now. It was very easy to decide that I simply couldn't be bothered, when getting going was such a fuss. Also, people interrupted me all the time.

ACTIVITY 26

While I now don't have to cope with these unfavourable study conditions, *you* may be forced to. How can one cope with such conditions? Write down some suggestions for how I could have coped better — give me some advice as to how to manage *without* a place to work.

These are the suggestions my colleague Alistair made:

1   Talk to the other people who share the space and come to an arrange-
     ment about when you can study *quietly* and when you *don't* need
     peace.
2   Put all your study things together in a box or something so you can
     get them out quickly when you need to.
3   Find somewhere *outside your home* where you can study regularly
     — at the local library or at work, for example.
4   Do it all early in the morning before others get noisy.

You probably thought of several other ideas.

4   Setting myself targets and deadlines

For a long time now I've been working with relatively few short-term deadlines
to meet. I may need to write a report by next month, a chapter by next term or
a book by next year, but seldom do I need to get something done *immediately*
— until I run into my deadline, or course, by which time it has sometimes been
too late. So I have got used to setting myself deadlines. I may ring up my
colleague Alistair and arrange to discuss a chapter of a book with him the following Thursday. That *forces* me to read the chapter, which I might otherwise
let slip (it also gives me a useful *purpose* for reading the chapter — now I will
need to look for points to make to Alistair, and think about the likely opposing
arguments he will make). I may make an arrangement with my secretary,Barbara,
to give her a report to type next Monday morning. If I don't produce the report
I'll throw her work schedule out and she'll give me a rough time! These devices
may sound a little contrived, but I'm really not a very self-disciplined person and
external pressure does seem to help me.

Such deadlines are less useful when I am working on a part of a much larger
task. I may know I've got twenty essays to mark by next Wednesday, but that
may not help me get down to marking the first batch this evening. The bigger
the task I face, the harder I find it to get stuck in. To deal with this I used to set
myself a working week — of thirty hours for example — when I was a full-time
student. This may not seem very much, but I had terrible trouble meeting it. I'd
do anything to clock up the hours. I'd doodle on my pad, and balance on two
legs of my chair, re-read what I'd written half a dozen times — anything to add
up the time to thirty hours a week. If I set myself two hours in an evening I'd
find myself looking at my watch all the time and leaping up from my desk the
moment the second hand swept round to mark the end of exactly two hours.
Setting myself targets in terms of *time* was hopeless. I hated it, and I didn't get
much work done.

Nowadays I set myself targets in terms of *tasks*. I decide to let myself watch
the England game on the TV as soon as I've finished marking two essays, or I let
myself go to bed as soon as I've finished reading a chapter. I end up putting in
about the same amount of time, but with much less effort and to *far* greater

effect. I find it very easy to keep going to the end of a task compared with keeping going until the end of an hour. Setting myself task targets requires that I have a fair idea of how long a task is going to take me. If I decide to mark six essays at a sitting and they turn out to take forty minutes each instead of the expected twenty minutes each, then I'm going to lose momentum as I imagine myself burning the midnight oil. I find it best to lower my targets rather than work towards depressingly distant or unrealistic ones!

5   Knowing when I work best

I've found I definitely concentrate more easily, and think more sharply and creatively, in the morning. I can keep at jobs for longer, and distractions such as a break for coffee, breakfast, a phone call, or bathing the baby don't stop me in my tracks, but still allow me to get back into my job immediately afterwards. I'm hopeless immediately after lunch — sluggish and without any great application or concentration. In the evening, if I can get going, I can sometimes plod along quite well — but the *quality* of my work isn't as high, and I'm more easily tempted by distractions and find it harder to get back to work after a short break. Whereas I can take all the short breaks I want in the morning without endangering the rhythm of my work, if I sit down to the *Nine O'clock News* on TV I have a devil of a job getting down to anything afterwards. There are some jobs I *can* do at night, if absolutely necessary; such as reading through something I've written and correcting spelling, punctuation and grammar — or writing it out more legibly for my secretary. People differ enormously in their work rhythms. Andy, a colleague of mine, can work well through the night, and is not very bright first thing in the morning. And I once met an Open University student who had got up at 6 a.m. for the previous five years in order to get her studying done before her household came to life each morning. I've had to experiment for quite a while to realise that I'm not like either of these people.

A number of points seem worth making about how I get organised:

- The way I work is clearly different from that of others who, for example, may find self-discipline, organisation and application relatively easy to achieve.

- I have arrived at the way I work now as a result of trying lots of things out and also doing lots of very *un*successful and *in*efficient things. I've noticed what seems to work and what doesn't and let that guide me.

- Although I've been improving in this area for years, it is still an everyday problem for me. It also seems a problem for everyone I've ever talked to about it. Talking to others about my laziness and lack of organisation helps me to put my problems into perspective.

- Paying attention to being organised and getting down to work has been of enormous importance to me. I find it all too easy to let things slip and to get behind with my work.

- Finally, there are very real limits to what I'm willing to do about working hard and being organised. I lead a relatively chaotic and haphazard life and adhering to a strict timetable or work schedule is more than I could face. I know it is *possible* for me to be more organised and efficient, but I'm not willing to do what would be required — it would mean too great a change in my life-style.

ASSIGNMENT F
The assignment for this unit requires you to look at your present ways of getting organised, getting down to it, and sticking at it, and to think about how you are going to cope with these issues. Are you going to have to make changes in the way you organise your life? What main problems and pitfalls do you foresee? Try to write 500-700 words about the ways you organise your studying and get your studying done. Write to your tutor so that he or she will be able to picture the way you work and so be able to offer comments and advice. I have included examples of two students' attempts at this assignment together with their tutor's comments. The tutor's comments are worth paying careful attention to here because the two students have tackled this assignment in rather different ways, and the tutor believes one way to be rather more useful to the student than the other.

ACTIVITY 27
These two students are clearly very different people with different lives and different ways of approaching everyday problems. This has resulted in them choosing very different sorts of solutions to the task of getting organised. Which of these students are you most like? And which solution seems to you most likely to fit your personality and style of life? After reading through each of these two students' descriptions, make a list of the ways in which you are similar to and different from them, and draw a few conclusions about whether their solutions are suitable for you. For example, I made these notes from reading Mrs Kirkup's assignment:

	Mrs Kirkup
Similarities to me	She's haphazard, she benefits from social support — important, she's pragmatic and flexible.
Differences from me	Her family life is more demanding, her spouse is less understanding, she has poorer study conditions, and she's more *determined* than I am.
My conclusion	Mrs Kirkup's situation is much more difficult than my own, although her temperament is similar. I don't need to go to such lengths to get work done, though perhaps I will need to become more determined if my family grows.

Here is Mrs Kirkup's assignment:

436 Acacia Ave.,
Neasden,
London, N.13
December 2nd

Dear Paul,

I've kept up my record of being later than I intended with every assignment — sorry about that, but better late than never!

I really got quite worked up writing this assignment. My desire to get
back to studying is causing me all sorts of difficulties at home, and simply
finding the time is my biggest problem. An hour spent reading a book
sometimes seems like an hour stolen from my family — especially from my
husband — and when the pressure is on I just have to give my studies a
miss in case there is a row. I hope you've got some bright ideas!

As this is my last assignment, I just want to say how much I've got out
of this course, and especially out of writing to you, and all your help. I'm
very grateful. I only hope all this effort won't be wasted.

Best wishes,
Mrs Jean Kirkup   307515

Mrs Jean Kirkup   *307515*   *Learning to Study*

Tutor: Mr Paul Johnson
Assignment F

Getting organised, getting down to it, sticking at it
My main problem with studying is simply finding the time. As you know, I
am a full-time housewife with three children, two under five, and before I
started trying to study this took up *all* my time, from morning till night.
My husband John has recently started a new job and he often gets home
late, tired and rather irritable, and I'm pretty well left to cook, clean up
and put the kids to bed on my own. At weekends John wants to spend
time with me and the kids, or goes off to watch football and leaves me to
look after them, so even at weekends I'm not alone.

I've heard about people having their own study — quiet, well lit, desk,
and books on the wall — but that is just a pipe dream for me. There isn't
enough room in the house, and the kitchen table is my desk. It's noisy,
and there is nowhere I can keep my books or papers. The kids have often
disappeared with my pens and paper — Ben, my youngest, even ate my
notes on 'Kes' once (I'm studying 'The Arts — A Fresh Approach').

So much for the problems. What do I do about them? I've found I can
do *some* reading standing up, whilst ironing, or waiting outside the school

for Jane. This isn't ideal but it all adds up. I've got into the habit of always taking the current novel I'm reading with me — I dip into it on the bus or in the doctor's surgery. For more prolonged study, when I need to concentrate, I've found it impossible whilst the kids are around. It's never more than a few minutes between a cry, a minor disaster, an argument, or mealtime. So now I do one of two things. The first, when John is here, is to simply take the car a mile away and sit and study in the car, leaving John with the kids. I got this idea from a play on TV and it's marvellous except that John is usually in a filthy mood when I get back, so I'll only take the car when everything is nice and calm at home. My second solution was to persuade Pauline a friend of mine, who also has three children, to study the same course. It's often chaos when I take the kids round to Pauline's and we don't get round to doing much concentrated work. But I find it a tremendous support to be able to talk to her about what I've been thinking about and I don't know whether I could have kept it up without that.

I haven't made any long term plans at all as I can never tell from one day to the next whether I'll even be able to get my books out, let alone stick to a schedule. But getting down to work is absolutely no problem at all. I can get totally absorbed in seconds and feel that if I ever had hours at a time to study I wouldn't lift my head for a second, I get that wrapped up in what I'm doing. You'd have to drag me away from my books.

I can't see things getting much better until all the children are at school during the day, which will be another three years. I don't think John realises I intend to apply to the Open University then.

27 Finsbury Park Road.,
London, Nw.
December 6th

Dear Jean,

Thanks for your last assignment. As always I found it easy to imagine your study situation from the way you write. Your sentences are getting much less convoluted, and this is the best structured piece you've written for me — though it tails off rather weakly at the end.

I must admit I hadn't realised the difficulties you worked under — it's not surprising you've taken so long to get through this course! It is a credit to your perseverance that you've managed it at all.

Some of your difficulty in finding time to study seems to be due to the social organisation of your household. Is there any possibility of your doing a deal with your husband so that he shares looking after the children more? I sense that he may be rather hostile to your studying. At present you may be able to struggle along, finding a few minutes here and an odd hour there, and taking as long as you like to get through the course. But in the Open University, for example, you will need to put in substantial blocks of studying on a very regular basis or you will get hopelessly behind very quickly. This will obviously require a more systematic allocation of your time than at present. Changing the way you use your time, as opposed to slipping a little studying into a largely unchanged life, may require more support and understanding from your husband and your children.

Your arrangements with Pauline seem an excellent idea and I hope you can continue to gain support and an opportunity to talk about your ideas in this way. This may not be sufficient as a substitute for such support within your own household though. How about Pauline coming to your own house, or even encouraging your husband to start studying?

You haven't yet encountered any problems getting down to wor or sticking at it partly, I suspect, because you have had little study time to choose between and because without deadlines you have never *had* to get down to your studying. You have always let your own deadlines slip quietly by. Again the Open University has fairly rigid deadlines, and you will often need to read or write when you don't feel quite like it, just in order to meet these deadlines. It's when you can''t afford to leave things till next week that getting down to work may become a problem. Try fixing in advance a time when you will study for two hours, and see whether it feels any different starting work.

I've enjoyed reading and commenting on your work. I hope you do go on to further studies.

Best of luck,
Paul Johnson

Here is the second student's assignment:

Flat 12a,
Brittania Buildings,
Orme Street,
Benfleet,
Essex.

13th October.

Dear Mr Johnson,
Please find enclosed Assignment E and additional timetable sheets.

Yours sincerely,
P. R. Higgins
Student No. 159207

Mr P. R. Higgins   *Student No. 159207*   *Learning to Study*

Assignment F

1) 'Learning to Study' has taken me two hours per week for six week , plus two hours per assignment for six assignments.

2) 'Introduction to the Computer' requires twelve hours study per week for twelve weeks, including twelve assignments.

The following plan was devised to accommodate these requirements.

Week	1	2	3	4	5	6	7	8	9	10	11	12	13	14	15	16
Date	15/9	22/9	29/9	6/10	13/10	20/10	27/10	3/11	10/11	17/11	24/11	1/12	8/12	22/12	29/12	5/1
Unit	1	2	3	4	5	6										
Assignment	A	BC	D		E	F										
Hours	4	6	4	2	4	4										
Introduction to the Computer — Unit (and Assignment)			1		2		3	4	5	6	7	8	9	10	11	12
Hours			12		12		12	12	12	12	12	12	12	12	12	12
Total hours	4	6	16	2	16	4	12	12	12	12	12	12	12	12	12	12

For next week, the week beginning 27th October, this requires the following allocation of time:

Timetable for week beginning Saturday 27th October

	6am	7am	8am	9am	10am	11am	12noon	1pm	2pm	3pm	4pm	5pm	6pm	7pm	8pm	9pm	10pm
Sat			Breakfast	SHOPPING	SHOPPING	STUDY	Lunch	WATCH SPORT ON TV				STUDY	Supper	SOCIAL CLUB			
Sun			Breakfast	▨	CHURCH	CHURCH	▨	Lunch	STUDY			Tea	▨	WATCH TV			
Mon		BREAKFAST	TRAVEL TO WORK (by train)	WORK (Teller at Halifax Building Society)				Lunch	WORK			TRAVEL HOME (by train)	SUPPER	STUDY		WATCH NEWS ON TV	
Tues		BREAKFAST	TRAVEL TO WORK (by train)	WORK (Teller at Halifax Building Society)				Lunch	WORK			TRAVEL HOME (by train)	SUPPER	STUDY		WATCH NEWS ON TV	
Wed		BREAKFAST	TRAVEL TO WORK (by train)	WORK (Teller at Halifax Building Society)				Lunch	WORK			TRAVEL HOME (by train)	SUPPER	Leader at Boy's Club		WATCH NEWS ON TV	
Thurs		BREAKFAST	TRAVEL TO WORK (by train)	WORK (Teller at Halifax Building Society)				Lunch	WORK			TRAVEL HOME (by train)	SUPPER	STUDY		WATCH NEWS ON TV	
Fri		BREAKFAST	TRAVEL TO WORK (by train)	WORK (Teller at Halifax Building Society)				Lunch	WORK			TRAVEL HOME (by train)	SUPPER	Parish Council duties		WATCH NEWS ON TV	

▨ Reading Sunday Newspapers or doing household chores

27 Finsbury Park Road,
London, N4.
October 28th
Dear Mr Higgins,
   Thank you for your final assignment. I am very impressed by the way
you have managed to keep to the schedule you have set yourself and to get
your assignments to me exactly when you say you will.
   I hope you have managed to keep up with your much more demanding
computing course. I wish you well with it.
   I have made a number of points concerning your assignment on the at-
tached sheet.

Yours sincerely,
Paul Johnson

Assignment F   *Getting Organised*   *Mr Higgins*

Your organisation and forward planning look truly impressive and show a
great deal of awareness of the overall time commitments involved in your
studies. However you haven't told me (i) whether your plan *works* —
whether you have found you can actually stick to it; (ii) *why* you have
planned your work in this intensive and highly structured way; (iii) how
your plan fits in with the rest of your life.
   There are a number of questions I would like to ask you before I could
say with confidence that your plans are likely to be very helpful to you.
Perhaps you could write down your answers and send them to me in a
letter. Firstly, concerning your overall plans:
1)   Why have you chosen to complete a unit (of either course) in each
     week? It is perfectly O.K. to take longer if you are pressed.
2)   You have not given yourself any weeks off — even over Christmas!
     Do you think you will be able to keep up such a pace without some
     leeway?
3)   Your plan committed you to spending *sixteen* hours in weeks 3 and
     5. Was this necessary or wise? Could you not even out your work-
     load a bit or have worked up to your peak load more gradually?
     Your plan to tackle the *first two* units of your computing course
     over *four* weeks seems a good idea, but perhaps you might have
     started in week 4 instead.
4)   While your timetable for week 7 (Oct. 27th) is an 'ideal' plan, you
     have already experienced a sixteen hour week in week 3 (Sept. 29th).
     How did this week actually work out? Did you manage to do sixteen
     hours or was it impossible?
5)   Do you intend to do *all* of your computing course — or are there
     parts you are already familiar with, not interested in, or will find too

80

difficult to attempt? Your plans might take this into account.

I also have a number of points about details of your impressively organised weekly timetable:

1) What did you do with your Monday, Tuesday and Thursday evenings before you started studying? How do you feel about losing all your evenings in this way?

2) You spend ten hours a week on the train. Can you use this time for any aspects of your studying?

3) You only have one hour, out of twelve, planned in the morning. Do you work best in the afternoon and evening?

4) It looks as though someone must be preparing your meals and keeping house for you. How does this person feel about supporting your studies in this way?

5) Do you find you are able to, for example, get down to your studies straight after lunch on Sunday and stick at it till five o'clock, just because you have timetabled yourself to? What happens when you feel bored, reluctant or tired?

6) Is your TV watching invulnerable, or would you give some of it up if you were behind with your studying? Will you feel resentful at having so relatively little 'time off'?

There are also some more general points I'd like to bring up:

1) As you have timetabled all your studying to take place at home, I assume you have somewhere suitable to work. Are there any problems about studying at home, for example on Saturday morning when things are usually fairly busy, or on Saturday evening when there may be some pressure on you to be more sociable?

2) Has your life always been very regular and organised, or are you currently attempting to become more organised? If your timetable looks rather full and rigid to you, don't be too surprised if you can't keep to it!

The overall comment I have to offer is that you may have been tempted to take on too much, too soon, and to structure your life in an organised way you are not used to. This will almost inevitably lead to some disappointment as you fail to keep to what was initially a perhaps unrealistic schedule. Don't be ashamed of working up to a regular heavy workload more gradually. You may also need to be more flexible in order to allow leeway for set-backs (e.g. 'flu' or just plain loss of momentum from time to time.)

If you do send me a further letter it would help if you could be more descriptive of your studying as you experience it — warts and all!

Paul Johnson

These two students have offered very different sorts of descriptions to their tutor. Mrs Kirkup has given a vivid account of her difficulties and practical details of her everyday struggle to get some studying done. However she hasn't given any account of her longer-term orientation — how long is she going to take to finish her Arts course? Do you think she has any idea what tasks need doing next, or which tasks she intends to complete in the next week? She certainly doesn't describe any such plans.

In contrast, Mr Higgins is exceptionally precise in his overall plans, but didn't make any sort of comment about whether they are useful, what sort of problems he has experienced in keeping to his plans, or what he might attempt to do about these problems. While the plan and timetable gave his tutor plenty of clues about which questions to ask, they didn't give him much idea how Mr Higgins actually got down to work.

The tutor made fairly bold comments about Mrs Kirkup's and Mr Higgins' home lives. Perhaps these may be seen as a little intrusive, or even impudent, but you would probably agree that their home lives have a very great deal to do with how they are likely to manage as students. You will have to give your tutor some lead as to how far you are happy to discuss such issues.

EPILOGUE

Now you've finished this course, what do you do next? What else can you do to prepare for studying? Ther are three main things I think you might bear in mind:

1. This course deliberately *hasn't* gone into some very specific aspects of studying, like taking exams, taking notes, reading and so on. These things are nevertheless important, and you *can* learn how to go about them more effectively. The National Extension College has a variety of courses which tackle these 'study skills' topics. There are also a large number of cheap paperback books with titles like 'How to Study' which cover the same topics. My own favourite of these is by Derek Rowntree and called *Learn How to Study*, published by Macmillan.

2. Most courses not only expect you to be able to study, but expect you to know something about the subject matter of the course too. An 'A' level maths course will assume that you already know about the maths taught at 'O' level. 'A' level French assumes you already know a certain amount of vocabulary and grammar, and so on. Some subjects, while they don't make assumptions about what you already know are, nevertheless, easier to study if you've done something like it before. For example, while you don't *need* to study any social science before taking the Open University's Social Science Foundation course, it certainly helps! The National Extension College offers a number of such courses which *introduce* you to particular subject areas. The best way to prepare to study social science is probably to study some social science!

3. Improving as a student doesn't necessarily require special courses. During this course I've tried to encourage you to examine your own study abilities and to pay attention to *how* you study rather than to *what* you study. When you are actually studying physics, arts or whatever, it is very easy to get bogged down in the subject matter itself and forget that *how* you are studying is also important. I hope that you will now be able to take a pace back from your books from time to time and simply ask yourself:

    'Am I going about this in a sensible way?'
    'Am I doing the right things first?'
    'Am I being evaluative?'
    'Am I explaining myself clearly in my writing?'
    'Am I studying in the way I know I learn best?'

    and a hundred other questions which this course has raised. Improving

83

yourself as a student comes about largely through paying attention to *how* you study and *why*, and thinking about this. If I've encouraged that habit, then I've done all I could hope for.

Good luck with your future studies!

Graham Gibbs